THE NEW INVESTOR'S GUIDE TO OWNING A MOBILE HOME PARK:

WHY MOBILE HOME PARK OWNERSHIP IS THE BEST INVESTMENT IN THIS ECONOMY AND STEP BY STEP INSTRUCTIONS HOW TO ACQUIRE AND MANAGE A PROFITABLE PARK

BY LAURA COCHRAN
WITH A SPECIAL FORWARD BY PARK INVESTOR ERIN COCHRAN

THE NEW INVESTOR'S GUIDE FOR BUYING A MOBILE HOME PARK

WHY MOBILE HOME PARK OWNERSHIP IS
THE BEST INVESTMENT IN THIS ECONOMY
AND STEP BY STEP INSTRUCTIONS
HOW TO ACQUIRE AND MANAGE A
PROFITABLE PARK

BY LAURA COCHRAN

With special thanks to

Austin, Sean, Erin,
Joe, Tony, Michal, Jonathon,
Liesl, and Kristie
for your professional edits,
support, and friendship

~ Thank you! ~

Cactus Flower Publishing LLC
P.O. Box 1545
Beaverton, Oregon 97075

Copyright © 2013 & 2015 by Laura Cochran

Printed and manufactured in the U.S.A.
ISBN-13 978-0-9842435-3-2
ISBN-10 0-9842435-3-4

http://www.mobilehomeparkinfo.com

IMPORTANT DISCLAIMER
INFORMATION TO FOLLOW

TABLE OF CONTENTS

A SPECIAL FORWARD BY ERIN COCHRAN

Welcome to The New Investors Guide to Owning a Mobile Home Park. My name is Erin Cochran.

Mobile home park ownership is the best investment in this economy. In a moment, you are going to receive step by step instructions and advice along the way how to acquire and manage a profitable park investment by author and multiple park owner, Laura Cochran.

My personal road to mobile home park ownership began when I was very young. I started modeling when I was two years old, working for Columbia Sportswear, the Bon Marche, Hanna Andersson Clothing, Adidas, and Banquet Frozen Foods.

But I didn't buy a park right away. When I was 10, I was actually more interested in buying stocks. So like many of you, I invested a lot of my earnings in the stock market. This was in late 2005.

I did very well in the beginning. I bought Mattel stock right before Christmas because I saw a number of my friends buying American Girl dolls. I bought pizza stock right before the Super Bowl.

Then my stocks started to lose money. There was talk in the media that some of my stock had lead in the toys. Whether or not this was true, just the perception drove my stock down. Even though I was only ten, it was very frustrating to watch my stocks lose money day after day. I had to find a more stable place to invest that would protect my initial earnings.

I made the decision: I moved my entire portfolio into investing in mobile home parks. Unlike my stocks, my park interests started paying me back immediately from day one.

That was 7 years ago. Not only have I earned a 58% return on top of my money, but my initial investment has also doubled because the park's value increased after I bought.

Parks are valued on several cost approaches, one being the value of the land they are sitting on, another being the income approach. That is why even in soft economic times, that parks keep their value and increase in value because the income is always there, and you increase the rents over time which means the cost approach valuation increases as well.

This may not be the best news since some of you are looking for good buys. They are out there, and this guide will show you how to recognize and identify them. but for he most part, mobile home parks are a stable and strong investment. Do not look for huge decreases in the prices of mobile home parks even when times are tough, because park owners know that the rent comes in even when the economy is down. Rent income keeps the values of the parks up. Parks are a good solid investment, now and for the long run. They will always increase in value because they are assessed on income approach, and the rents always go up.

You do not have to be a model like I was, or even need to have seed money to buy into a park. As hard as that sounds to believe, the lady I am going to introduce you to is a single mom who bought three of her multiple mobile home park properties using credit cards for down payments, which she paid off with the rents from the parks.

She started investing in and managing her real estate when she was 24 years old and by the time she was 29, was a self-made millionaire from real estate investments and from the passive income from the mobile home parks, and has been buying parks ever since.

Wherever you are in life, whether you are just starting to think about investing, or wishing you had more to show for retirement, Laura Cochran, my mom who I would now like to introduce you to, can demonstrate how buying a mobile home park investment is the best answer for producing monthly income for every investor.

Wishing you success and continued investing!

INTRODUCTION

This investor's guide is dedicated to everyone who has ever questioned the soundness of his or her financial future. Millions of Americans have found themselves getting sea sick as the stock market has grown increasingly risky.

If the stock market is a vehicle, then riding in it is a lot like holding on for dear life: you are bouncing around in the passenger seat, and when you look over, there is not even a steering wheel. At best, you and all the other passengers, can buckle up and hold on for the wild, bumpy ride over which you have no control and are not really sure where it is going to end up, or what you are going to have left of your vehicle when you finally get there.

The only thing you can really do as an investor in this situation is pick the vehicle. Once you get in, you may or may not arrive safely based on past performance and unknown contributing factors.

This illustration seems to cast the stock market as an unsafe, irrational, and somewhat schizophrenic way to invest.

With few other options and their life savings in jeopardy in a volatile economy, retirees likewise cannot count on social security for sole support when it comes time to retire.

Some retirees or those close to retiring from the public sector, such as teachers, police personnel, and firefighters, now find themselves living in cities and states that do not have the means to fund their pension promises.

As cited by cnbc.com in Pandemic of Pension Woes Is Plaguing the Nation: upon closer inspection, a survey by Pension and Investments, a trade publication, found that in 2011 the actual return over the last 10 years had averaged 5.6% per year – not the 7.84 to 8% projected necessary to fund pension promises of the top 100 largest public pension funds.

Headlines tout retirement propaganda, reminding the investor that it is never too early to start saving for retirement.

But the reality for many in our nation is that older persons, probably even some that you know or encounter throughout your day, must now continue to work well into their retirement years because they simply cannot afford to stop working.

According to some financial advisers, in order to retire at a comfort level- which is considered to be 20 percent below the present lifestyle of the majority of Americans - the retiree would need to have no less than $1 million dollars in retirement to produce the income needed to retire. Most planners will tell investors that number is closer to $1.5 or $2 million saved into retirement.

This is simply not attainable for many in today's economy.

What did some of our parents, or even our grandparents, do when they were planning for retirement? Many turned to investing in government bonds. But that plan does not work the same for this generation, especially when recent headlines post: Bond Losses at Federal Reserve Top $192 Billion. This recent editorial goes on to say that bond investors are "getting hammered." Although it could be debated that these losses can play kick the can down the road and not manifest until the central bank decides to sell and incur actual losses, the point remains, that the federal government should not be any investors last resort.

Retirement accounts require income and discipline on the part of the investor. The typical investor may have experienced a change in his or her work environment, including restructured schedules, cuts in hours, reduced pay, and possibly even being laid off. The disciplined investor must set aside a substantial percentage of his or her income to begin the growth process of the retirement account. Sometimes investors get started later in life, and must hope for better returns, which do not come.

Ominous headlines remind investors of phenomena, such as high-frequency stock trading, the effects of Quantitative Easing, central banking's stimulus programs, effects of a European recession, and flash crashes in the stock market itself. Other articles muse that the Asian markets are trying to tell us something of a pending market crash. And still more experts say to plan for worst case scenario and that another crash is inevitable, saying in interviews that there *will* be another crash.

If choosing from the array of risky stock investments were not challenge enough, the investor in this arena is already starting from a disadvantaged position.

Most retirement accounts are grown with after-tax dollars, so already the investor is investing from a lower dollar amount to begin with.

The investor must decide which aspects of daily quality of living must be sacrificed in order to infuse large percentages of his or her income to make the investment account grow. The investor has no control over the market. There is no guarantee that there will even be money from growth, or the entirety of the initial nest egg remaining in the retirement account when it is actually needed.

Some accounts experience catastrophic losses from sources other than market volatility. There are corrupt companies and corrupt brokers in whom investors have entrusted millions, only to lose everything.

Many retirees are no longer able to retire as planned. They must keep working to keep up with rising health insurance premiums and other daily encumbrances, unplanned and largely unforeseen during the early working years.

Retiring investors have not been the only casualties of a tumultuous economic terrain. Entire states and countries have found themselves in financial straights, via overspending, over-borrowing, or natural disasters.

Unpredictable and dramatic swings in the stock terrain on a national and global economic front have further alarmed investors. Unprecedented debt has caught the attention of the entire globe as nations scramble to bail out their contemporaries.

Even sadder is the economic reality that many simply cannot afford to invest because new jobs, for example the 162,000 jobs that the economy added last month, were of a poor, deficient quality offering only part-time employment and low wages disproportionate with the skill-set or financial needs of those seeking the jobs.

According to a recent post by Associated Press, "Part time work accounted for more than 65 percent of the positions employers added...Low-paying retailers, restaurants and bars supplied more than half (the) job gain."

What is the answer? What is the solution and the best investment alternative for this economic picture?

Mobile home parks are the key to successful investing for many park owners and investors. Although it has been a well-kept secret, it is not a surprise.

With all this negativity surrounding the investment arena as you know it, it is significant to remember that you have an alternative that has worked for many exiting the broken vehicle.

Alternative investing has caught the attention of many savvy investors. Many financial advisers have started steered clients toward moving money out of the market and investing heavily in real estate. Not even a year has passed since the Business Market headlines, "Wall Street Pounded, Nasdaq Hits Correction Territory," falling 10.7%.

But simply moving assets into real estate is not enough. The problem with investors divesting and diving into the real estate market is that most investors have little or no experience, and have no concise idea how to make money in real estate. Their adviser's idea is not for the client to *make* money, so much as to prevent further losses in the stock market and stabilize the investor's portfolio.

The rationale behind moving investment dollars into real estate is simply that no more land is being made. Real estate is a finite commodity and will always be in demand because it is a limited-supply market.

But investing in the real estate market is a labyrinth: there are so many choices, and many of them are mine fields of unprofitability.

Should the investor buy a single-family dwelling to rent out? As soon as the one tenant moves, the investor faces a 100 percent vacancy factor. Likewise, if an investor purchases a duplex, one vacancy equals a 50 percent vacancy factor in which the investor must cover half the expenses. These are no longer profitable situations for an investor.

Additionally, stick-built rentals, as they are called, are maintenance-intensive ventures. Becoming a landlord ushers in a slough of habitability issues that the new owner must address regularly, and not always at convenient times.

However, the secret for the new investor is to invest in Mobile Home parks, trailer parks, RV parks, or a combination of all of those parks.

Mobile home park ownership is attractive and desirable, offering one of the best investment opportunities on the market. Unlike a stick built rental, tenants rent the ground from you. And although tenants can break many things, it is almost impossible for tenants to break the ground or the dirt they are renting from you, known as a space. The investor is renting out spaces, and collecting rents on only the land. This is a fantastic investment alternative for someone wanting to move their retirement into stable monthly income.

Mobile home parks make sense from a cash flow standpoint because the investor multiplies the rents by the number of spaces in the park and can see the gross income each month. After subtracting out several predictable expenses, it is easy to see how much money the investor will have left over each month. This is a predictable income. Fluctuations in mobile home park income are in the control of the investor, who can fill vacancies and keep the cash flow steady.

Affordable, safe housing that is found in mobile home parks is always in high demand. Not everyone makes money owning a mobile home park, which is why there are so many parks available for purchase. This how-to manual will steer the investor through the process of using analysis to calculate how to turn a park profitable.

Mobile home parks frequently enjoy a zero percent vacancy factor. Many tenants live in parks by choice because it provides them home ownership on a scale that does not involve them paying property taxes and they feel at home in a park community. Mobile home park living is a great stepping stone for young families saving for a down payment or for single persons who seek the privacy their own home provides that they cannot find in an apartment situation.

Park settings have turned out to be ideal for persons who wish to stay in their own home independently and are trying to avoid nursing homes, but still want people around to check on them. Parks have also turned into a wonderful alternative to higher functioning persons with disabilities who want independence and are not comfortable in a group home, but will function with great success in a park neighborhood.

In summary, purchasing a mobile home park is in my opinion, and based on my own twenty years of real estate and mobile home park investing, the best alternative investment for the serious investor. I think every investor should own a mobile home park, and here is why:

- Low to zero vacancy rate
- Steady monthly income
- Predictable monthly cash flow
- Good return on investment
- Investor has control over cash flow and vacancy rate
- Additional opportunities to increase cash flow through rent raises and eliminating utility bills via pass-through billing
- Mobile home parks hold their market value and appreciate in value
- There is always a demand for affordable housing found in parks
- You retain your initial nest egg that you purchased the park with – your investment dollars are in tact

My hope is that my twenty years of hands-on experience in the rental and mobile home park industry synopsized in this how-to manual will help guide your park investment experience.

My situation was very extreme and compelling that drove me to research thousands, and ultimately purchase a number of mobile home parks. Many years ago, I found myself a single parent because my child had just become severely, permanently-disabled. I decided that my child would always have a place in my home, but I had to find the most effective means to deliver a stable and dependable monthly cash flow to pay for my son's expensive and continued care for the rest of our lives, and even after I am gone.

Whatever your personal motivation, buying and maintaining a profitable and successful park should be rewarding and financially stabilizing for you.

Whether you are purchasing a park as your sole investment, or adding parks to your investment portfolio, park ownership is a commitment on several levels. You will either be interfacing with your new management team; or dealing with tenants directly yourself, tenants who may try to test your patience and educate you in all aspects of landlord-tenant law. You are committing your time and integrity as you balance running a profitable business venture with ethics in maintaining your rents and doing your part in the role of affordable housing. You will have situations where you can make a lot of money; but you may also encounter opportunities to help someone less fortunate than yourself, who has maybe had few breaks in life. Only you will be able to make those decisions as they come.

In return, you will emerge financially sound and secure, collecting monthly profits, financially calm and unscathed by the rest of the globe reacting to changing economic tides. You will have the distinction of being a landlord who owns mobile home park investments.

The affordable cost of living offered by your park is one of the basics of human existence – food, water, shelter – people must always have affordable housing, so you will likely enjoy full parks, often times hopefully with a waiting list to get in to your park.

Your investment into a mobile home park is stable and time-tested. Owning a mobile home park will provide you peace of mind that your investments are no longer at the whim of unpredictable economic times and mysterious market fluctuations, over which you have no more control than a passenger being flung around in a vehicle without a steering wheel.

As you follow some basic, common sense steps to researching and vetting your new park investment, you will be rewarded with immediate monthly returns on your investment, and the stability of park ownership. Your investment will retain its value, and more likely appreciate in value, as you enjoy predictable, dependable monthly income for the remainder of the time you own your mobile home park.

Here is to wishing you all the best with your continued success as you begin this life-changing adventure!

CHAPTER ONE
W.O.W.
Working for Your Money, Own Your Own Business, Your Money Working for You

The interesting thing about money is that you do not have to go to a job every day for the rest of your life to receive income. That is called *active income.* Active income means *you* have to stay healthy and engaged in your career and show up at work in order to actively produce income.

The power of money is that it can also be put to work for you. It does not even have to be your money working for you either that is creating more cash flow and income that you get to keep. When money flows into your life every month through other means, it is called *passive income.*

I do not believe in retirement. I believe in solid, dependable, stable, passive income that comes into your life every single month for the rest of your life. Retire today. Retire never. Wouldn't you like to have that option? It is all up to you. Finding ways to create passive income for yourself gives you freedom and stability by making money work for you.

The acronym W.O.W. stands for
- **W**ork for your money
- **O**wn your own business
- your money starts **W**orking for you.

W. stands for Work:
You work. You get a job and work for your money. Your employer pays you, you pay taxes, and your employer pays taxes on you. Your employer tells you when to show up to work, and you do. It makes no difference if you are working as a burger chef or a top salary engineer; you are still actively showing up at work and collecting a paycheck.

You can also work for yourself. Under this W, work is work. Even if you are working in your own profession, you are still working to earn a paycheck. This means you are actively going to a job and performing a service in your profession to earn a paycheck. Under this W. in the W.O.W. concept, you are an active earner.

Active self-employment could be any profession: an accountant, an attorney, a doctor, a laborer, a contractor, a consultant. These people, even though more independent than fast-food or box store employees, still have to get up in the morning and go to work in their chosen professions.

O. stands for owning your business.
To be hugely successful in life, the success that really separates you from all the other hard working people in the world, you are going to have to own your own business. Can you really ever be richer than the person you are working for? Do you see your boss paying you more than he pays himself? Even if the only business you ever start is the LLC that "does business as" (d.b.a.) your mobile home park, that is a critical, hugely important step to becoming financially independent.

Owning a business or multiple businesses is going to be key to your bottom line when tax season approaches. Business owners are able to itemize and deduct legitimate business expenses. For you, this means your properties will be opportunities for business expenditure write-offs that you deduct from your income. This puts more money back in your pocket and maximizes your cash flow.

Do you know how much you pay in taxes if you are working for active income? Your take-home pay reflects that taxes have already been taken out. Next, should you be lucky enough to earn profits on your stock market investments, you pay taxes on the earnings. Should you withdraw funds from your conventional retirement fund, you again pay taxes. You are paying taxes continually on money that has a lower earning potential because it has previously been taxed every step of the way. No wonder people have no money left to work with, or invest, and so many people are living paycheck to paycheck.

You have to pay your taxes; I am not advocating otherwise. But you need to be smart about the tools the government has in place for you to maximize your earned income. Two of the greatest vehicles the government has given you are the opportunities to own your own business and invest in real estate. You need only sit down with your tax adviser to be informed of the many tax benefits of these two ventures. That is why I want you to do both: I want you to start your own business investing in real estate.

Many purchases for your business and for your rentals are purchased with *before*-tax dollars. This is huge news for you. Then you are able to take deductions for these purchases necessary for your business off your earned income and reduce your tax burden that much more.

W. stands for working for you.
Your money working for YOU.
The final W. of my system is where money goes to work FOR you through a continual stream of passive income. If you are ever going to achieve freedom from worry, stability in your finances, or flexibility in your work scenario, you are going to have to maximize your passive income.

The best part about putting money to work for you is that you do not have to invest money that you have had to earn and save. There is no other industry that I can think of where your intelligence and responsibility are rewarded with other people's money like they are in the real estate industry.

Have you ever had a bank say to you or your parents, "You have done such a great job showing up for work and staying late all these years, we want to loan you money to invest in your retirement account."? I do not think so. Or have you ever heard, "You are such a hard-working citizen, we want to loan you money to invest in the stock market!"

This is not the society we live in. You and your parents invest money left over after raising families with the hope those funds will grow in the stock market, after which you pay more taxes on the earnings. Even persons earning social security are taxed at a certain point on their social security income. What an insult to be taxed on social security in some cases, after one has finally reached an age to receive it.

It is different in real estate. There are actually transactions that happen completely devoid of taxes. This protects 100 percent of your investment capital. You would never get that in the stock market! When you sell a property and make a huge profit, you are actually able to roll the entirety of those profits through a 1031 tax exchange into an even-more valuable, higher-priced property.

How long would it take you to earn $1.5 million dollars for your retirement? Only you know the answer, but it took me less than five minutes to secure $1.5 million dollars for two mobile home parks I recently purchased. Not only did I put the bank's money to work for me, but those two properties alone gross over $18,600 each month, which makes the payment to the bank with money left over.

The money left over after the bank payment is my passive income that will be there for the rest of my life. The mortgages will be paid off in less than twenty years, at which point I will capture an additional $7,500 in passive income on those two properties. This does not even take into consideration future rent raises, which will increase the net monthly income on those properties anywhere from $6,000 to $15,000 per year.

All of this comes from money that I never technically earned: it was handed to me by the bank to invest and manage in real estate.

I really want to encourage you to move your energy toward finding ways to increase the passive income flowing into your life. That is what this book is all about, and the most efficient means I have found for doing that for you is by investing in mobile home parks.

CHAPTER TWO
TYPES OF PARKS

There are several types of parks for you to choose from.

MOBILE HOME PARKS (MANUFACTURED HOUSING COMMUNITY):

consist of single-wide manufactured homes, double-wide manufactured homes, and, very rarely, triple-wide manufactured homes. Newer mobile home parks will be comprised more-heavily of double-wide homes. Lenders like to see a larger proportion of double-wide structures in a park because it is harder to move a double-wide, and that means more stability for the lending institution.

TRAILER PARKS:

can consist of manufactured structures and a mixture of travel trailers. Manufactured homes are difficult to move, so a lot of people prefer a travel trailer, recreational vehicle, or a fifth-wheel trailer. The most attractive feature of travel trailers is they can be moved on the freeways with a simple trip permit or current tags if they are under 40 feet long. The same can be said of what is called "park model" homes, which are truncated manufactured homes that can be moved by a semi-truck or hauler with a simple trip permit from your local Department of Motor Vehicles (DMV), because these units are shorter than 40 feet long.

RV (RECREATIONAL VEHICLE) PARKS:

typically an RV park is an overnight facility where travel trailers, campers, recreational vehicles, RV's, and fifth-wheels pull through for the night and camp anywhere from a day to a week. After a week's time, campers will be asked to convert to a week-to-week rental agreement. Campers who remain longer than 30 days should be converted to a month-to-month rental agreement, at which point they are considered "permanent RV's" or long-term tenants.

Investment in RV parks is not something I recommend unless you are planning on living and residing full-time in your new RV park as your own on-site manager. In an RV park setting, if you do not live inside your RV park, it will be difficult to know how many trailers are in your park at any given moment.

If you are really planning on living and residing full-time in your new RV park as your own on-site manager, then in this scenario you have likely just bought yourself a job, which may work for some investors.

But if you are in investor hoping to keep your investment at arm's length, you might consider RV park ownership as a lot like owning a bar: a lot of cash changes hands. If you are not going to be there 24 hours a day, someone is going to be collecting this money for you. This increases your exposure and the likelihood of being stolen from.

I don't wish to offend the many honest RV park managers, but since I am having a conversation with you as the investor, I am telling *you* as the potential owner of an RV park, to please keep in mind that owning an RV park that takes overnight tenants --as opposed to month to month tenants-- may expose you to theft and loss of cash revenue which you may have needed to cover the expenses, but now you are short and still have to pay the bills.

In an RV park setting, if you do not live inside your RV Park, you are never going to know how many trailers are in your park at any given moment. You will never know if the tenants paid you. They may have paid your manager, but you may never see that money.

What if an RV pulls in because they "only need to sleep for a couple hours"? They'll be gone by morning. They don't need to use your dump station or hook-ups. A manager could say, "Thirty dollars, pull in over there." Might it be possible that the over-nighter is not going to show up on any rent roll that you're ever going to see?

Some members of my professional team, who I analyze park projects with, recently commented to me about a park we had toured where the manager had a large number of trailers that were not showing up on his monthly rent roll report to the owners. The off-site owners, who were trying to sell this park, lived five hours away and were losing thousands of dollars each month in revenue. They had no idea why, and they were in the middle of divorce, so they had other things on their mind. The owners had no way of tracking how many trailers were in their park at any given time.

These owners suspected someone was stealing from them, but had no idea how. They could not get their books to balance and were paying thousands out of pocket each month to cover the park expenses which they were subsidizing by working other jobs.

Meanwhile, their on-site manager wore a considerable amount of large gold jewelry, owned five nice cars, a yard full of ATVs and riding lawn mowers, two large pickup trucks, several boats, and kept one of the park storage facilities full of his hobby-mining equipment.

To discourage dishonesty from an on-site manager, you could possibly install security cameras or utilize an online security company to host a web site with your cameras that you can monitor online from your location. But if you are being stolen from, you are never going to have all the money on the table to account for.

There are just too many opportunities in a cash transaction for you to be sure. You might stop some of the theft with cameras, but you are not likely to know what the rental arrangement was. Perhaps the tenant was told one hundred dollars, out of which you see twenty.

In my experience with site security cameras, there are blind spots and low resolution issues from long wire runs. System maintenance leads to downtime when your system is just not going to be functioning, from repairs, storms, cable installers, your local power company, dump trucks, or your local squirrels tearing into your lines.

I have installed several park wide surveillance systems, and, ironically, over time, every single camera has been stolen, no matter how many feet off the ground, by a well-meaning tenant, service contractors from phone or internet, stolen by one tenant who didn't want to get caught dealing drugs, removed by another tenant who figured out how to install them on his own trailer claiming he was watching the park for me! So I do not recommend a security monitoring system as a way to keep track of over-nighters or keep a manager honest.

If you are certain that the best property available to you at this time is currently accepting overnight tenants, you might ask a trusted friend or family member to help you oversee your park during the times when you cannot be on-site. You might want to switch as many of your spaces as possible as soon as possible to monthly tenancies.
Another consideration if you are weighing a traditional mobile home park versus an RV park may be the maintenance of public bathrooms. This might not sound like much, but public bathrooms

can become a nightmare. Not only do public bathrooms invite loiterers and transients, but you may be required by laws in your state to complete yearly safety inspections with your local health department.

Another consideration if the park you are looking at has publicly accessed restrooms is if those bathrooms are in ADA compliance, approved for the Americans with Disabilities Act. This may also pose a problem for you, keeping your public restrooms in compliance and providing safe, accessible, and marked parking for same. This invites costly renovations and updates at your time and expense, which will not net you any more income on the cash flow side of things.

The other problem with public restrooms in your RV park is that they are public, which means everyone from the community where your park is located can also access your restrooms. And what do restrooms have that every household uses? Before long, you are providing toilet paper and paper towels for not only your entire park, but, more likely, for your entire county.

I analyzed a park's books several weeks back, and observed their expenses for toilet paper and hand towels for just the first four months of their fiscal year had already cost them over $2,000.

Again, these issues surrounding restrooms are not problems for park investors who choose a manufactured housing community, as opposed to a recreational vehicle facility that accepts over-nighters.

If you purchase a park that has month to month tenants and restrooms, it is your choice to lock the bathrooms. All homes located in your park come self contained with their own bathroom. You are not required to provide this service to your monthly tenants because they are only renting a space from you. Some parks that have on-site facilities as a courtesy for park staff have gone the route of locking their restrooms, and issuing a pass-key.

If you are still weighing a manufactured housing community investment versus a recreation vehicle park that you have found, another consideration is who is going to clean the restrooms. If you are not there daily to clean, you would need to hire someone to clean the restrooms, at a minimum of several times per week. During peak season, public restrooms need to be cleaned daily. Hiring out the cleaning may cost in the hundreds of dollars per month.

And the final consideration why I would encourage first time park investors to seek manufactured housing communities over recreational vehicle parks is that RV parks are seasonal. Three to five months out of the year you may make a lot of money, but the rest of the time, the revenue stream will be a lot slower.

The true benefit of getting into a park is the stability of the monthly cash flow, and you will not necessarily capture that from a park of over-night activity. There are many RV Parks on the market. If you look closely at the listing pictures, you may see green grassy knolls and very few trailers. When you go to look at the park, the listing agent may tell you that it was full this morning, they had twenty trailers just pull out before your arrival – but this type of park investing is a gamble and not ideal for new park investors.

I recently returned from driving through ten western states, and observed many unoccupied and dark RV parks. So when you are shopping, please be mindful to analyze at least twenty-four to thirty-six preceding months of cash flow, and not just the booming summer months that will not represent to you the big picture. The reality is, there will still be a hefty mortgage payment on an RV park even when there is no income, so I wish to help you avoid a bad situation by steering you away from RV Parks, and towards manufactured home parks and trailer parks full of month-to-month tenants.

Mobile home parks and trailer parks with long-term tenants will provide you the most-steady monthly income. If after your searching parks you do decide to purchase an RV park, you might consider living on-site and encouraging long-term tenancy to stabilize your monthly return through the slow season months.

CHAPTER THREE
WHERE TO FIND PARKS FOR SALE

Even though I am in my early 40s, when I first started researching my own rental investments and mobile home park properties, twenty years ago, the only place to find listings were in newspapers and local real estate booklets, and by networking with commercial real estate brokers to please call me if anything came available, and by calling the parks themselves, and their owners, through the yellow pages. My cell phone was the size of a shoe box and took up the entire center console of my car. I bought one of the first digital cameras to log my real estate research, and the camera cost over $1000.

Obviously a lot has changed, but these are still some of the best ways for you to find parks before any national or global investors become aware of parks for sale, in your particular area.

Mobile home parks are relatively unique to the United States. As a result, I have met investors from around the world who have come to my How

To Own a Mobile Home Park investment seminar at the Trump International in Las Vegas.

In asking these investors a little bit about themselves, I have met park investors from the Middle East, New Zealand, Australia, Israel, from across Canada, and from the United Kingdom. In addition to these buyers, you are also competing against American investors who are interested in purchasing a park investment.

A simple internet search will find you all the same park listings that they are looking at, on popular park listing sites. These are my personal favorites:

- mobilehomeparkinfo.com
- mobilehomeparkstore.com
- loopnet.com
- cimls.com
- birchrealty.com
- rmls.com

Please don't be discouraged by the competition. I believe that there is a mobile home park, or multiple parks, in your future. You are going to see different opportunities such as maybe you are the investor willing to fly every other month to the 200-space park in South Dakota because it has a 28% return, and no one wants a park in South Dakota. Maybe that is your golden goose to buy where no one else wants to buy.

Maybe you are willing to buy parks in Texas where the parks come with a lot of additional acreage. Or maybe you are willing to travel to Florida several times per year to purchase a large property that is under-performing.

In just a few chapters later in this book, you will be able to identify what issues in a park you feel qualified to fix, and turn most any park profitable for you. I say FOR YOU because I do not want you to share your good ideas with the sellers, or with the listing brokers, or there is a chance the park will not stay on the market when they themselves implement your good ideas and now find themselves running a profitable park.

Early in my investing days, I was purchasing a small 30-space park on the West Coast which I thought would double as a vacation destination for me to take my family, since they like to ride ATV's on the coast.

The sellers were older, and their children could not stand the park. No one had visited the owners in the park for years.

There were a number of tourist-based services in the town, so I immediately identified several ways to attract new tenants; I also mentioned I intended to auction and sell the park-owned homes which were costing the owners thousands each month in maintenance repairs.

My commercial loan was approved, for only 10% down because that was not uncommon at the time, so for about $30,000. Then suddenly all communication ceased. I could not get a hold of my sellers. My bank was anxious to fund, the title company was ready to paper and close the deal.

No one knew what had happened and the sellers would not respond to my many messages left on their machine. The listing was pulled and everything went dark. On a hunch, one day I called the park about three weeks later, and sure enough the children of the owners answered.

The children had suddenly developed an interest in running a now profitable park, implementing my ideas that I had shared with the sellers.

Fast forward several years, the children called me to see if I would still be interested in purchasing their park, but now the price had more than doubled, and was listed at over $700,000. This time it was me not returning their many calls. By then I had already bought several other parks and after that, kept my ideas to myself.

The Internet is the first place to research mobile home parks for sale across the nation, in all 50 states. There are also often regional and local multiple listing services which service smaller particular areas, usually no larger than one or two adjoining states. You may need to call several realtors to find out this information for your particular state.

My favorite search engine for mobile home parks is of course my own website of listings across the United States, at

http://www.mobilehomeparkinfo.com

As soon as you visit mobilehomeparkinfo.com, you are welcome to email me via the CONTACT US email located on the website. If you put CHAPTER THREE in the subject line of your email, I will give you a FREE SIX MONTH membership for free unlimited park browsing across the United States.

Please just go to mobilehomeparkinfo.com

Another web-based nationwide mobile home park resource is

www.loopnet.com

The park listings can be found by clicking on For Sale, then scrolling down to Search By Property Sub-Type, then selecting Mobile Home / RV Community from the Multi-Family listing.

Regional park listings can be found in the Northwestern United States at

http://www.rmls.com

To find the mobile home parks on the site, enter the page through Quick Search on the left, then click on the Commercial tab at top center. Next, scroll down the drop-down menu to Mobile Parks.

By searching for mobile home park listings per state, you will also discover a number of pocket realtors who specialize in park listings for their particular area. One of my personal favorites is a Florida based real estate company whose colorful website is:
www.daytonavisit.com/hotels-mh-park.htm

Local business classifieds for your newspaper will also be a good resource for tracking parks for sale. These do not always appear daily. Sunday is the day those listings appear in smaller newspapers, in the business classifieds listings for Mobile Home Parks.

Very rarely, you will find mobile home parks listed on www.craigslist.com under the businesses for sale. This is a time-consuming and potentially pointless search, since you have to weed through a number of states and cities to even see if there are any parks listed. But sometimes parks do show up on craigslist, and even on ebay, although I have never purchased a park from either of these sources.

The best source for finding mobile home parks before they ever reach the newspapers or Internet is to cultivate a group of commercial listing brokers who specialize in mobile home park sales. Brokers work for you for free and get paid on commission when a property sells, so they are very motivated to help you find the property that best fits your scenario. Let them know you are interested and ready to buy a park, and exactly what you are looking for. Request packets of all their park listings that are in your price range.

Some very motivated commercial brokers will even generate a letter or postcard, at their expense, advertising to all the parks in your entire state, that there is an investor ready to buy that park, are they willing to sell at this time.

Even if this is not a service your commercial broker has ever done, I would encourage you to please ask any commercial brokers you know, if they would be willing to give a shout out via postcard, or letter, or on any other marketing circular they are mailing, to all the parks in your area. You are a solid buyer, and the broker might get a mobile home park listing, and sizable commission, out of the deal. It is absolutely worth asking a broker to do this for you.

I receive multiple solicitations every week from commercial brokers, just sending me a postcard or a letter, seeing if I am willing to sell any of my parks. The postcards say any version of the following– we have cash buyers looking for Mobile Home Parks; we have exchange buyers looking to spend up to $3.5 million and aggressively looking for parks; or, out of area park owners and investors are looking for additional park investments if you are willing to sell your park.

Brokers you connect with will also continue to email you listings weekly or monthly, or whenever something specific comes available per your criterion. They will also put you on their mailing lists if they send out updated listings of parks for sale throughout the year.

If you are looking to buy a park near where you live, you might stop in and visit all the parks in your area. You might inquire about their vacancies and how much they are charging for rent. And just start asking questions if the park might be for sale, if it is one you are interested in pursuing.

Instead of driving by, you can also call the property. Park managers especially often really enjoy talking to someone who is interested in their property. You might also research your local parks at your county through the local tax assessor's office. This will tell you what the property taxes are, if the tax payments are current, or if the property is in distress and the sellers might wish to sell.

You will be surprised that by calling every single park that interests you, something may come available. The situations will surprise you because they are all different. Sometimes, parks never even make it to market because someone like yourself was waiting in the wings and simply expressed interest like you are doing.

On a park I called on recently, the property owner had just passed away, but someone else had their eye on the park and had already made arrangements to purchase the park right out of the family trust outside of probate. That is a park that never even got listed before it sold.

Even if you discover that a park you are interested in has an offer pending, you may wish to find out how long ago the offer was submitted, and if it has been accepted. You can always write a back-up offer to purchase a property, even after there are other offers in the queue ahead of you, and even after an offer has been accepted.

This puts you in first position if the buyer ahead of you fails to perform or defaults on any of his contingencies during the purchase process.

Sometimes park buyers submit multiple offers on a number of parks at the same time, then research them and simply terminate the offers that are not as favorable to them. If you are next in line on that park, you will then move into first position as that property becomes available.

It is also acceptable for you yourself to send an unsolicited letter to the owners of a park that you wish to purchase, even if it is not on the market.

Identify yourself as an investor who is interested in purchasing their park if they are interested in selling. Include your contact information, and they may contact you if they are considering selling.

If you are a member of a large club store, such as Costco, you might look into getting yourself a toll-free phone number for about $5 per month, that permanently forwards to your phone or cell phone, and gives your callers about 60 free minutes per month if you wish to provide a toll free phone number for sellers to call you back on.

Another strategy for finding parks before they go to market is by meeting park owners where they gather. I live in a state that requires four hours of continuing education for park owners or managers, every two years, and these classes have been another networking opportunity to meet managers or owners who are selling or who know someone who is selling a park.

You may wish to enroll in these classes yourself, just to meet park owners and find out what is going on in your state before you purchase.

It is not uncommon to meet future investors who are auditing or paying to take these continuing education courses to find out what is going on currently in their state's mobile home park world, and to start to make those connections with other owners before buying a park themselves.

These classes can be found by contacting the mobile housing community in your state.

So, in summation, your best resources for finding mobile home parks for sale are as follows:

- local newspapers or realtor circulations
- commercial brokers local to the area you want to buy your park in
- commercial brokers willing to solicit you to all the parks in the state you want to buy in
- national internet searches, including the popular park listing services:
  - mobilehomeparkinfo.com
  - mobilehomeparkstore.com
  - loopnet.com
  - cimls.com
  - and occasionally craigslist and ebay
- regional smaller listing bodies such as rmls.com and daytonavisit.com

- by contacting directly, all the parks you like, to see if they might be interested in selling to you
- and by attending your state's continuing education classes for park owners and managers if this is something your state offers

CHAPTER FOUR

WHAT MAKES A PROFITABLE MOBILE HOME PARK?
Cap Rates And Cash Flow

Unlike stocks or investing in someone else,
park ownership is an investment in you. You have
ownership and control over your own rent
collection and income situation. You are not
holding your breath or losing sleep about how your
investments are doing. You already know what the
bottom line will be each month.

To investors who do not know about owning
mobile home parks, the typical a scenario of
someone investing for example $20,000 would be
to invest in an array of retirement products – stocks,
bonds, mutual funds – do some research, invest the
money and go away. There would be some fees and
taxes. The investor checks the pulse on the
investment along the way to see if there is a
different number than he or she started with. Oh
look, it went up $17 today! Then perhaps the next
day, oops, lost a lot today. Should I buy more while

the price is down? Wow, up $114 today! Down $900, how can this be? The seasickness continues.

Maybe after a year of this type of investing, the investor's hope is to have earned about $133 per month, or about an 8 percent return on the initial investment. A solid, predictable 8 percent annual return on investments for the rest of the investor's life would really please most investors.

More likely, you have not made $133 per month. You may have even lost money, a lot of money. There are fees, there are taxes, and there are losses beyond your control. You did nothing wrong except buy the wrong product, listen to the wrong friend or adviser, or just have a run of really bad luck with whatever company, economy, foreign market, or chip industry. It seems like those facilitating the products you buy are making more money from your money than you are.

It does not really matter what you invested in, because at the end of the year, you know exactly what you have left over. It is not really a whole lot to retire on, not now, and maybe not when you need it. You are investing in hope, needing the market or situation to improve, you are not sure how or when, but you need it to at some point down the road for this whole scenario to work well. So you put in more and more of your hard-earned money.

Here is an alternative. Take that same $20,000. Say you can leverage that $20,000 into something in the range of a $200,000 park. Now you are investing with a whole lot more dollar power than with your own $20,000. What bank is going to give you that $180,000 you just borrowed if you told them you needed it to play in the stock market?

No bank loans money for you to invest in the stock market. There is a reason banks loan on mobile home parks. They are a solid return for your and now their dollar. If you buy on the West Coast, you will get about six to seventeen spaces in a $200,000 park. If you buy toward the Midwest or Southeast part of the country, you will get a lot more spaces in your park, possibly closer to 20 or 30 spaces depending on what markets are doing.

So let's take the average. Your new park has about 18 spaces. Let's figure average space rent; again, on the West Coast for example, space rent averages between $300 to $400 per space, in the outlying areas, closer to $140 to $175. So now, your little 18-space park is bringing in about $270 per space. Multiply those together, and you are collecting $4,860 per month. Out of that, you are going to pay your mortgage (about $1,200 per month on a seven-percent 30-year mortgage with $20,000 down).

From your $4,860, you have subtracted your $1,200 mortgage and probably paid water/ sewer, insurance, trash, and common area lights. For an 18-space park, you are probably looking at about $1,174 for those bills. Save out your property taxes, which will likely be between $200 and $400 per month, and you are looking at the following: $4,860 minus $1,200 mortgage, minus $1,174 utilities, minus $400 for taxes = a little over $2,000 each month, in your pocket. This is your net take-home pay from your park, your passive income each month for the rest of the time you own this park.

If you want to net more passive income each month from your parks, you may choose to purchase a larger park, or perhaps several parks.

Obviously, there are going to be some parks that you look at that are not profitable. But those reasons are all within the owner's control and usually something that can be repaired to make a healthy, profitable park.

But for now, let's just look at the return on your investment. If given a choice between earning $133 per month on your $20,000 or making a much larger return of closer to $2,000 per month, I think you would choose the better return. Not only that, but the $133 is not guaranteed. You might lose $133 in a month. But the park income is stable, predictable, monthly, and you have the law on your side if you have to collect any rents that do not come in to get you to that $2,000 bottom line.

What about in 20 or 25 years when you have your park mortgage paid off? Now that $1,200 you have been paying each month is yours in addition to your $2,000 and you own your park outright. Likely, at this point, instead of $3,200 per month cash flow, that will be a higher number. What if your rents are no longer $270 per month, but you have increased them $10 or $15 every couple years, so now after 25 years your space rents are $340 or $360 per month? Now your take home is somewhere between $4,500 and $4,900 on your same little park.

The way I figure cap rates or return on investment when I am crunching numbers on a mobile home park may not be how the selling realtor finds cap rates. I am not into fancy formulas and email attachments full of current and projected cap rates and pro-forma textbook gibberish. Does the realtor own mobile home parks? These numbers are designed to make the park look better than it is. The selling broker is trying to sell you what the park could be doing. If it could be performing easily at that level, would not the current seller be doing so?

The selling broker is going to tell you reasons why the park is performing poorly, or how it would amazingly transform into these fantastical numbers under his formulaic calculations. Take those into consideration, but here is what works for me:

- What is the price of the park?
- What is the number of spaces?
- What are the rents charged per space?

Let's take the example we just used of the $200,000 park with 18 spaces charging $270 per month. I multiply 18 x $270 x 12 months, and divide that by $200,000, so about a 29% return on your money. This is what I consider a cap rate for myself, my return on investment. There are realtors who would largely disagree with me, but my formula is very simple and I am looking for a number that is in the high teens or higher. On this particular example, your rate of return is about 29%.

Are you getting a 29% rate of return on your current retirement portfolio? Are you seeing that rate of return on any of your investments? And keep in mind, that 29% rate of return is not even on your own money. You only brought $20,000 to the table. Your little personal rate of return is closer to 291%. And you are going to get this rate of return on your money, on your bank's money, on your entire property *every single month for the rest of the time you own this property*. This is what makes mobile home parks such a desirable investment. This is why mobile home parks stay in families for generations. This is why investors keep parks for their children and grandchildren tied up in trusts and estate planning for generations.

You are going to have vacancies and you are going to have down time when you are making repairs. The secret to minimizing the impact that is going to have on you is by having more units. The bigger the park, the better. The more units you have, the less you are going to feel your vacancy factor.

If you only have one unit such as a single-family home that you are renting out, you are going to be impacted by one vacancy because that is 100 percent of your rental income. If you have 80 units, what kind of an impact is one vacancy really going to have on your bottom line? We are talking about a one- percent impact: one divided by 80, $400 divided by $25,000. You are not going to feel a one- percent impact like you are going to feel 100 percent. Owning more units is a better scenario for you, for your bottom line and financial stability.

How do you know what type of cash flow you can depend on from your park? Here is a little crib sheet for you to use to figure out if your park will produce cash flow:

CHAPTER FOUR
What Makes A Profitable Mobile Home Park?

CALCULATING YOUR PARK'S ABILITY TO PRODUCE CASH FLOW:

Price of the park:_____ (a)
Number of spaces:_____ times amount of rent per space:_____ = _____ (b)

Multiply (b)__ times 12 (months per year) = ___(c)

Divide (c) by (a) = _____ this is your park's temporary cap rate, your rate of return, your expected return on investment (look for a number in the high teens or higher; what do you need to get that rate of return? A lower asking price? More income on the rent side? Is this reasonable for your area?)

Now we need to find your monthly take-home. What bills is the park paying? Fill those out here, *only* the bills the park (you) pays:

What is the water/ sewer bill:_____
Common area electric bill:_____
Trash bill: _____
Insurance:_____
Property taxes:_____

TOTAL: _____ (d)

(b) minus (d) = _____ is your expected monthly take home pay.

Now it is time to look at the parks real expenses. Remember that park owners are going to write off a lot of expenses, and they might not be running this park like you are going to.

Look at their numbers with the knowledge that you are probably going to be making some changes. Why are they paying $18,000 per year for maintenance? Is that an expense you can expect, or what are they doing differently from how you might run this property? Do they have a dishonest employee charging them hourly for things you are going to look after yourself? Why are they paying $14,400 for year for lawn mowing, when there are only five little postage-stamp lawns in the middle of the park? Are they paying cable? Are they paying an office phone? You can reasonably expect to eliminate many of these frivolous expenses.

Maybe there are expenses you do not see that you *will* see if you are not careful. Have the huge old trees, sprinkled around the park, been maintained? How much is removal of dead trees going to cost you? What about that old roof on the office building? What is that going to run? What about that old water system that has not been touched in forty years? What about a sewer system that was installed out of orangeburge[1] sewer line back in 1950 that only had a five-year life expectancy? How much is that going to cost to replace to 76 units?

You will want to secure at least several contractors' bids on all the big-ticket repairs you can imagine. These are going to help you reach a reasonable price for your park. I always purchase assuming worst case scenario. If I can find a park that cash-flows well, even in the worst conditions

[1]

"orangeburg" is the brand name of bituminous fiber sewer pipe that was manufactured by the Orangeburg Manufacturing Company, this sewer pipe material was constructed from rolling tar and roofing material into the shape of a tube. The bituminous material tends to break down and deteriorate as it ages. Next, the pipe begins flattens out and the interior circumference is no longer round. Flattened pipe can further be damaged by router tools. The pipes are very penetrable by plant and tree roots. The roots grow along inside the pipe and eventually block the flow. These problems show ups as repeated backups of the sewer line.

imaginable, then I can be assured in the good times I will have a financially healthy park

Ideally, you are going to get to a point with your park where the above formula (b) minus (d) is what you are taking home each month. You have control over that number. In many cases, you have the ability to negotiate lower expenses and raise rents. Run several scenarios and see if this park is going to cash flow for you.

CHAPTER FIVE
FINANCING
How Can You Afford A Mobile Home Park? How Can Anyone?

One of the greatest misconceptions of mobile home park investing, is that ordinary people cannot afford a mobile home park.

If someone has decent credit, this could not be further from the truth. Investors get discouraged by different friends and family members who argue with them, saying "With what you have to put down for a down payment, you are not going to get much of a park! Who are you kidding? You could never afford a mobile home park."

I would not be writing this book if I did not believe that everyone with decent credit and good moral integrity has the potential to get into a mobile home park. It is much more attainable than you think. How many lenders have your critics and discouraging friends and family interviewed? The reality is that banks have a tremendous appetite for these types of properties.

I personally do not understand how a sophisticated investor could *not* afford to own a park as part of a sound investment portfolio. Parks in my opinion are the most secure and time-tested money making formula out of any investments.

Well-meaning naysayers are simply uneducated about how banks look at these parks. The parks produce income, and the banks count that income toward your purchase. The park must generate enough income to be self-sustaining, which is what you want anyway – a profitable park.

Mobile home parks are not break-even or lose-your-shirt ventures. Mobile home parks need to make you money every single month, or it is not the right park for you to purchase.

Over the course of meeting with clients and students looking at park ownership, I have met a number of younger investors who have little of their own money to work with, but they have brought together their entire family, or in some cases, multiple families and generations, to purchase a mobile home park investment because park investing makes so much sense.

In some scenarios, families are looking to purchase a park with whatever funds are left in the retirement account of an elderly family member whose care expenses in a nursing home are about to overtake their remaining funds, and then the elderly family member will have no more money and nowhere to live. It makes more sense in some scenarios for the family to invest in a park to retain all the remaining money, into the park which will retain its value, and then use the monthly rents to pay for the expensive assisted living care costs for the elderly relative.

Other clients and students have found properties where the sellers want zero down. These are not always the best scenarios for investors. Although these zero-down park-ownership deals are out there, I have never purchased any of the zero-down parks that I encountered since there are always factors to be analyzed; and my students had the same experience when getting into the details of the zero-down park opportunities they likewise found.

Just in the last year, an investor from one of my classes texted me and her fellow classmates, about an 8-space park being sold for $17,000 in Arizona, and no it was not a typo. The area was remote and not desirable to everyone, but those deals come along, and that may be a situation you find as you start researching and analyzing parks that you want to add to your investments. There was another fair-sized park in Oklahoma for $48,000, which is less than most people would pay for a down payment. So park deals can still be found, and you will create your own best case scenarios when you find a good-priced park and then identify a number of expenses you can expect to trim.

Even some investors with millions of dollars in the bank sometimes will not spend their own money, preferring to keep it stashed away, and using other people's money, or banks with low commercial interest rates, to finance their mobile home park investments. No matter what the interest rate the bank is charging, the investor has already determined their rate of return, even on the borrowed money, is going to be so much higher, and they don't even have to disturb their own cash to do so.

Commercial lenders are going to be looking at several things. They are interested in how you are structuring your offer, how much you are coming in with for a down payment, how much you want from them, what your financial health looks like, and what the cash flow from the park looks like on paper.

Right now, your whole focus may be *how much money do I have to have, to get into a mobile home park?* But the bank you are borrowing money from may just see that as part of the equation. The bank is also taking into consideration:

- How much exposure does the bank have on this park?
- What is the bank's risk of not getting repaid?
- How much can we sell it for if we have to take it back?
- What are the odds this borrower is going to make us foreclose on them?
- Do the monthly rents cover all the expenditures and the mortgage payment each month?

The goal is to answer these questions favorably for the bank when you meet with your lender.

A number of lending programs are in place that benefit park buyers. I will touch on several scenarios for conventional lending.

Government-based backing is a tool used by some park investors, and it could involve Fannie Mae or Freddie Mac, where your bank lending you the money requires a 20% down payment of the purchase price. If you use this scenario, and you are looking at a $200,000 mobile home park, you will need to come in with $40,000 down as a minimum; likely a little more for fees and closing costs unless you and the lender agree to roll them into the loan.

Other banks, not federally backed, will vary with what they require as a down payment. It is rare these days to find a conventional lender, except maybe a small community bank or credit union, who only requires 10% down of the purchase price to lend you the money, but you want to ask. It is more likely that conventional lenders will ask you to bring as much as 30 or 33% to the table so they can make sure you have some "skin in the game" when you are borrowing their money.

There is also a small business program (SBA notably through US Bank which is not in all states) that allows the borrower to only come into the transaction with 10% of the purchase price. This means if you were buying a $200,000 mobile home park, that you would only be bringing in $20,000 of your own money. This SBA program is federally backed which is one reason that the down payment is so much lower. But there are also criterion that have to be satisfied and the lender will have to tell you the requirements you will have to meet if you go with this particular funding vehicle.

In some situations, you might ask the sellers of the park if they would be interested in taking a second position subordinate to the bank. If you were coming into this purchase with 10% down, perhaps your sellers could account for the difference between what you have to bring to the deal and what the bank needs to see as a down payment, for example the remaining 20% to bring the bank's exposure to 70%, the seller's exposure to 20%, and your investment to 10%. In this case, the sellers would be receiving 80% of their entire purchase price – your 10% down payment, and the 70% the bank is giving them-- so this might be an attractive option for the sellers to get their park sold to you, since they just sold their park and already have received 80% of their asking price so they will be in a pretty good mood. Collection accounts for paying them the remaining 20% can be set up through a third party escrow, through which they would receive a monthly check, either mailed or direct deposited to them, according to the terms you mutually agree on.

In situations where the park is owned outright, free and clear by the sellers, they may wish to *be* the bank, and make arrangements for purchase with you directly. In this situation, you can tell them what you have available to put toward the purchase price and see if this is agreeable to both parties. They may even offer you a lower interest rate than the bank, and you will both benefit from avoiding costly fees and closing costs. You will want to protect yourself by having your or both parties' attorneys prepare and review the documents for the sale.

Maybe the sellers are only willing to carry a loan for you short term such as two to five years, at which point you would balloon the remaining balance of the purchase price that you still owe them, and you will ultimately end up in a refinance situation with a lender. It may be easier for you to refinance your park with a lender, than to purchase it outright if you are just starting.

The benefit of refinancing a park that you have been buying for a time from the sellers is that the bank will be able to see your management style and that you are seasoned with the property, meaning the bank will have a snapshot of how you are going to run the property so there will be fewer surprises for the lender if you are already seasoned in the property for the last several years.

Most banks structure commercial loans in several ways. You will have some options, but they will not vary that much.

- Regardless of your down payment, loans are typically amortized over a 25-year period. Your choices for other lengths of amortization could be as short as 15 or 20 years, or in some rare situations, up to 30 years. By visiting bankrate.com you can enter several payment scenarios into the mortgage calculators to see what your park income will support, if the park is bringing in enough to pay for its own mortgage.

- It is important to research different banks and which are going to give you the lowest interest rates, especially if this is a loan you are keeping long term

- There may be a diminishing or fully scored prepayment penalty built into your loan if the bank is offering you a low interest rate and wants to be sure to make their money back by keeping you as a customer for the next five years

- There may be a balloon payment built into your commercial loan; you will want to question your loan officer to find out what happens at this balloon juncture. Some lenders will fix your rate for five, perhaps ten years, at which point they will simply roll your loan to an adjustable rate until you relock it, which they will usually allow you to do within several weeks or several months grace period of the fixed rate expiration date; or the bank may want to use that juncture as a point to reassess your property. You will want to know their procedure and protocol before you commit to a loan with any bank. Some banks are very considerate at this point in your loan, and your loan officer will simply call you to see if you want to renew with them and proceed to re-lock it; other banks are predatory and will seek fees and paperwork and put up some other hoops depending on their mood and relationship with you, or if they have an interest in the property that you just spent the last five or ten years paying down the balance on. Just know going in that you will want to be prepared for whatever your bank has planned for you when the five or ten year fixed rate honeymoon expires.

- Inquire about points or what your closing costs are going to run. The best lenders are going to keep your fees around one percent of the total price of your loan

If you negotiate an interest rate that you are very happy with, you will want to fix your loan for as long as possible. If rates go down, you can always request a rate adjustment or refinance. If rates go up, you are in really good shape. It is safer to fix for longer. If you have questions about the differences, risks, and benefits, now is the time to ask your lender.

You will want to figure out what your monthly mortgage is going to cost your park. If you visit any of the multiple listing services you found your park on, many will have a quick link amortization schedule calculator on the site. To get specific with dates, rates and numbers, you can also refer back again to the mortgage calculators at

http://www.bankrate.com

Your lender may also post mortgage calculators on its web site.

<u>Ideas for coming up with your down payment:</u>

If you are sincerely wanting a mobile home park, but have little to no money available right now for your down payment, you might be trying to figure out how you are going to assemble your down payment. You might be thinking about all your options. Some ideas are to consider and re-evaluate your resources. Look around your financial plate with fresh eyes. Treat every available dollar equally. Here are just a few ideas that may be worth a closer look:

- You might consider selling or parting with some of your valuables or vehicles: consider short-term enjoyment versus financial stability for life. You can always buy yourself another car, and it will probably be a lot newer and nicer than your current model; if you locate a good deal on your mobile home park and are worried the property is going to get away, you may need to act quickly since the perfect park for you may not come along in your area every day.

- Lump sum from a job, settlement, or severance pay: where are you going to invest it before there is nothing left to show for it?

- Work more, earn more: if you are able, pick up a second job or work more hours at work to generate more income for your down payment.

- Spend less: budgeting works. Be disciplined and save for your park's down payment.

- Sell something: that second home, bare dirt, another rental property, something else you already own that is not really working for you or earning you a monthly return, or this asset has started costing you more than it is earning you.

- Emergency reserve: if you decide to invest it now, be sure to recommit to rebuilding it if you do not think your new monthly cash flow will cover an emergency.

- Put off saving for your child's college: I know this sounds harsh, but your intelligent child will have all sorts of funding options and student loans available to him or her. Can *you* get a loan for your retirement? Invest in yourself, and you will be doing you both a favor. When your mobile home park investment produces cash flow you will have the extra income to pay for your child's college when the time comes.
- Monetary gifts: is there someone planning on giving you a gift? Up to $14,000, a monetary gift to you is tax-free.
- Borrow from family: if this is an option for you, be sure to draw up a promissory note agreement to formalize this. Be an honorable borrower; always pay back what you borrow as soon as you can.
- Borrow from someone you do not know: private money can be very expensive, but there are several peer-to-peer lending groups surfacing now on the internet, such as:

www.prosper.com

www.lendingclub.com

www.upstart.com

www.fundingcircle.com/BusinessLoan

- Be sure to borrow responsibly, and have your attorney review your agreements as necessary.
- Sell any U.S. Bonds: do you have accrued or expired U.S. Savings Bonds? If you are just not sure, call 1-800-553-2663 or visit

http://www.treasurydirect.gov

- Overdraft lines of credit: if you have unused overdraft lines of credit sitting on the end of your free checking account, go online and transfer funds directly into your account. If your bank allows, this is one of the few places you can do a free cash advance. Write your check on your own account. This will also save any fees you might be charged for dipping into the overdraft without first transferring the funds.
- Credit card offers: these are a very viable source of money for your down payment. I have put down payments on several parks funded by nothing but writing myself checks received from credit card offers; be disciplined and always pay these off as soon as you can.

- Home equity line of credit (also called a HELOC): bank interest rates are very reasonable for temporarily tapping the equity in your home via a HELOC product.
- Unsecured loan (also called personal loan or signature loan because you secure it with only your signature): ask if the bank also offers and unsecured line of credit. This product has not been as readily available in this economy, but some banks still have these in their portfolio of products to choose from.

Keep in mind that your down payment might come from available cash, it might come from a business line of credit on a business you own, or it might even come straight out of your overdraft protection.

Only you know where you have money stashed and untapped credit. Only you know how important this investment is to you or how good of a deal you discovered. If you are not comfortable dipping into your credit, then you still have time to work, and save, until you have what you need to put down on a park. There is no rush; this is your investment.

You might also consider approaching your family about pooling their resources, even if your only contribution to the deal is offering to run the park for them. That is significant and your time, your knowledge researching and vetting park properties, and your people skill working with renters, are all resources that have value that you are bringing to the table.

Remember that you are shooting for a very low bar. Maybe you are looking at a $175,000 park with 17 spaces. What do you have at your disposal that adds up to 10 percent of $175,000? This number you need to reach is only $17,500. Or 20%, then you are only needing $35,000. Then, keep in mind that those 17 spaces are going to start generating revenue back to you the moment you close. The rents may be $350, so immediately you are receiving $5,950 per month from your new park space rents. Now how do you feel about that second vehicle you've been meaning to sell anyway? Or those tools, landscaping supplies, or collectibles that do not mean as much to you at this point in your life, as having the security the passive income from your park will provide. Maybe it is time to sell some Hummels or the dusty Corvette covered up in the back of the barn.

If you are considering your park as your primary investment but are not comfortable moving your retirement nest egg, then you can find a means other than your retirement savings to fund your first park. Work at your own pace and comfort level. Keep both parallel investments – your retirement nest egg and your park. There is no reason you cannot diversify and own paper, and tangible investments. Decide for yourself that which is the better return on your investment, your stocks, or your park. One will outperform the other, and it should be the park. But you should be the one to make that determination.

Maybe you actually intend to use your IRA, or self-directed IRA, or 401k as the funding vehicle for your down payment or park purchase. You will want to be speaking with your tax accountant and researching the ramifications so you know ahead of time if this is a good move for you.

What is your mortgage payment going to be on a $175,000 park when you put down $17,500 for 30 years at 6.5 percent? Approximately $995 per month. What else do you own that is going to bring in about $4,250 per month income on rents and cost you $995? And after 25 or 30 years, you have your park paid off. Not only do you keep all the profits, but now that additional $995 goes in your pocket. Some people receive less than that per month from their social security.

For that kind of money and stable dependable income every single month for the rest of your life, you can probably scrape together a 10 percent or 20 percent down payment. And this is just an example of a small park. There are much larger parks out there for not much more down.

When you are looking to buy your park, you may find that sometimes the only person who believes in you is *you*. You may get discouraged. You may even start to doubt yourself. But the reality is, you can do this. Investing in the right park for you is a decision that will reward you and your loved ones financially for the rest of your life.

If you are still worried about failure or running out of money, then imagine your worst case scenario on your number crunching of the property you are analyzing: i.e. what if eight tenants do not pay this month! You are welcome to use the park-analyzer CALCULATOR (you can find this tool located at www.MobileHomeParkInfo.com in the tools bar, up at the top), and enter a number of different scenarios, such as purchase price, and rent income received. If you find that your park numbers are still in the positive, then you will be reassured each month and pleasantly surprised when your park is full, and you have met or even exceeded your wildest financial goals.

You will get peace of mind knowing that you are in a proven industry: you are providing affordable housing. Most tenants are very good about paying their space rent, because they can't afford to move and pay another deposit somewhere else. If a tenant does not pay you rent this month, you issue them a notice that demands they pay you in 72-hours. The court is on your side that your notice gets fast-tracked through the FED system and you are standing before a judge with your tenant in just a couple weeks. Most tenants know this, and they don't want to move. Where else are they going to find to rent when there are already ten families lined up to take their spot in your park? So put your mind at ease, and take it from myself and thousands of other successful park investors, mobile home parks and RV trailer parks are most likely to be the best investment you will ever make.

Whatever your reason for wanting to purchase a park- to achieve family goals, financial freedom, stability in your retirement- you have reached the time in your life when you feel ready to start seriously researching a mobile home parks. You have decided this just makes sense, it is financially logical to purchase a park for yourself. Maybe you know someone who owns a trailer park, and they are doing enviably well. Maybe you have a friend who bought himself a park and he is now very successful and seems to have a lot more money, a lot more interesting hobbies and travel destinations, and happier than you have ever seen him.

Banks are going to be your biggest fans as you start looking at parks. Very few customers approach lenders about mobile home parks. Banks have a lot of interest in parks because lenders carry so few park properties in their portfolios of investments, so this is an area of interest where they make room in the interest of bank diversity of holdings. Obviously this depends on the bank, since commercial banks are not a one-size-fits-all, and not all commercial banks lend on park properties. You will just have to ask. But if your bank is interested in joining you on your park purchase, then they are going to be *very* interested.

Banks look at several things when you start looking for financing. They look at the property you want to buy, and they look at you. They are especially interested in the park you are considering. Provide them copies of everything you can get your hands on. They will want full rent rolls for probably the last three years, a detail of the park, copies of the bills the park pays, and a copy of your purchase agreement with the sellers. For the bank to get a good look at you, you are going to need to provide them, or fill out on their own form, something called a financial statement. It is basically a snapshot of your financial health. This shows the bank your net worth and lists your assets and obligations.

Your lender will likely require several years' taxes. These are not critical to your profile unless you are borrowing from an income-based lender on these properties. Taxes are not so important to equity-based lenders who look at your overall net worth when they are considering your credit worthiness. Your personal income from your day job, or even from your small businesses that you may own, does not need to be your strongest asset. You don't have to earning a ton of money, or showing a lot of income coming in from your job, because remember the bank is also going to be looking at how much income your park is bringing in each month. When you buy your park, there should be zero money coming out of your monthly paycheck to feed your park. That is not an investment, that is a nightmare. The park needs to make you rich, not the other way around. You are not a charity, you are not running a non-profit; you are a park investor who needs to make serious monthly income and returns on your investment in this mobile home park or permanent RV park. This park needs to have a clear path to making you rich, or it is not your park.

If you have found a lender that you want because they might be meeting a few of your targets like best interest rate, best terms, good location, you like your loan officer, etc but they require a larger percentage down: you can always consider coming in with a larger down payment.

If you are looking at bank-financing or credit-union-financing a park purchase, you will want to find out their minimum percentage down payment LTV (loan-to-value), but the very least you can expect to invest is going to probably be 10 percent. From here, you can figure out what parks are within your budget. If you have $20,000 to put down, you are looking for a park that is $200,000 or less. If you have $50,000 to put down, you are looking for parks in the price range up to $500,000.

Please do not try to figure out how a marginally surviving park might pay its bills, or try to shoehorn a local park into a hypothetical money-making situation. If a park is scaring you, then your lender is going to be scared, especially if this is your first park. Unless you can make a strong case for all the expenses you can reasonably expect to cut, the lender is going to look at this park's past performance, and perhaps your lack of experience. If the park has been poor for a while, you might start to wonder what else got neglected such as deferred maintenance or infrastructure concerns. There are much better parks out there. The lender wants and needs you to succeed, and it wants the park to carry its own weight and put money in your pocket every month. You want a park that is going to make you money. There are enough parks out there for sale for whatever reason, that it is worth taking the time to find the absolutely most profitable park you can find that makes sense for your situation (i.e. proximity, state of repair, price).

A small 20-space typical mobile home park should have, at a conservative minimum, at least several thousands left over for you as net income, after you subtract out all the mortgages and monthly expenses. If a park is not putting at least several thousand per month back in your pocket, it is not a good park for you. You will either want to figure out ways to get the expenses down, the rents up, and several thousand left over for you, or you will want to take a little longer to keep researching other properties until you find a decent return for your investment.

You can log a spreadsheet or keep a binder on all the parks you research so you can check back after you have analyzed a number of properties to see how all the numbers compare.

Finding park financing will be exciting for you as you discover the banks and the sellers, and maybe even your own family, who want to help you reach your dream of successful park ownership.

CHAPTER SIX
GETTING STARTED
Interviewing Banks

Interviewing banks is one of the cornerstones of running an efficient mobile home park machine. You need to determine which bank will be the recipient of all your park deposits. You are looking for a long-term relationship and will have this banking-deposit association for pretty much the entire time you own the park.

Ideally, you are going to establish a deposit relationship with the bank that funds your loan that finances your new park.

This may not be true in every situation, however. I have had at least five commercial loans on my parks with a bank that I have never made a rent deposit in, but they still loan me their money.

The bank you choose to deposit your rents into needs to be the best bank for you. You should interview at least ten banks. Many will be very similar, but there will be several that will really stand out above the others.

These are the two questions I want you to ask:
1. Do you offer a *free* business checking account?
2. Is there a minimum balance required for your basic free business checking?

You are looking for a bank that offers a free checking account and requires no minimum monthly balance because these are two less fees that you will ever have to worry about. When you have established the bank that is the best fit for you, you will want to open a free business checking account that does not have a minimum balance requirement.

Do not open this account in your own name.

This account will be set up in the name of your business. You will ultimately open this new account in the name of the business you are going to start, or in the name of the business you are going to purchase real estate through. This account should be totally *free.*

CHAPTER SEVEN
SETTING UP YOUR BUSINESS
The Value Of A Corporate Veil

Now that you have established your bank relationship, you need to name your real estate entity. You need to create a business name. Many mobile home parks are already named, but you are naming your company that will own the park and does business as the park (for example Smith Properties LLC dba Coffee Creek Mobile Estates). At some point, there is a chance the name you choose is the name your tenants, county, or insurance company are going to have to write on their checks. If you make it too complicated or difficult to spell, you are going to have problems with returned checks because the name is spelled wrong. If you are not creatively inclined, look around for natural ideas such as Shady Elm Properties, Prairie Dog Estates, Blue Sky Homes, etc. You can use acronyms of your or your children's initials.

If you are unsure if someone already has the name you want to use for your business, check online with your Secretary of State's office. You can search the Internet under the key words "filing in (name of your state)" or "business name search (name of your state)."

There is one category of new businesses that you will want you to focus on: Domestic Limited Liability Corporations. All this means is that your business name is going to end with the initials "LLC" (for Limited Liability Corporation). This means exactly what it says: an LLC limits your liability. If for any reason your company ever gets sued – and I say your company because you are now protected under the corporate veil of your LLC, so you are not getting sued personally—that LLC will limit the extent to which you will be at financial risk.

To be in business for yourself, you have to have that Limited Liability Corporation protection. It costs typically anywhere from $40 to $100 to register your name as an LLC, depending on which state you register in, and this is the first investment you will want you to make. You are also welcome to research the tax differences in your state that an "S-Corp" corporation, or incorporating your business, might offer. You will want to get the maximum liability protection for your new property.

Once you register and pay for your name, you own it. At this point, you can print your proof of ownership from the Internet and take it to your bank. Your bank can use your state's web site to track the ownership of your company to you, and you will be able to open your new bank account in the name of your new LLC. You have not given up any control of your business or given up any access to your money. You are 100 percent or full owner of your business, the property it buys, and the income the real estate will earn you. You have simply dropped an invisible shield between you and the rest of the business world.

This initial investment of $40 to $100 is very inexpensive insurance. You, your family, and the assets you have earned in your lifetime are worth this simple protection. At this point, you do not need to apply for a federal tax identification number since you will be using your own social security number on your tax returns as the single member LLC. Should you ever get to a point where you wish to add payroll employees, you will want to revisit the subject of applying for a federal ID number with your tax preparer.

If you have heard that forming an LLC is a costly, time-consuming process, it can be true. Having started and owned numerous LLCs, I can tell you that in my experience, between setting up an LLC through an LLC attorney versus applying myself online, there has been no legal difference. But there was an enormous cost difference. The LLCs I formed via the online registration cost me $50 apiece, the LLC through the business attorney cost me over $1,800. The difference was that I paid him to file the $50 process fee and have his secretary draft a version of my articles of organization.

You will need to register your LLC with your state, and you need to complete an operating agreement for it to be legitimate.

CHAPTER EIGHT
YOUR PROFESSIONAL CIRCLE

When you get to a point at which you are serious about investing in a mobile home park, you are going to need to surround yourself with your personal network of experts, individuals you trust in each of the following career categories:

- Banker
- Lawyer
- Realtor
- Maintenance team or handy person
- Professional adviser
- Tax accountant

These individuals are crucial to your success long term. Professional friends have a stake in your success: you pay them for their guidance and wisdom and education, and they have a professional interest in your well being and success. Once you have a circle of professional friends from each of these key careers, you are going to learn together by talking and working through whatever scenarios you encounter.

When interviewing attorneys, choose a firm that has senior and junior attorneys on staff. The benefit is that the senior attorneys will assist you in court but their rates may start around $240 per hour and range upwards of $600 per hour. The younger attorneys, just out of law school, charge a fraction of that – about $120 per hour. And you really get your money's worth. The younger attorneys still remember and practice textbook law. They can quote regulations to you all day long because they just passed the bar, regulations which you may need if you have to go to eviction court. Your state bar can also provide referrals for lawyers who specialize in park law or landlord tenant law.

In addition to legal counsel, it is time to find someone to loan you money. You have already interviewed banks. Now I want you to interview lenders. You may not necessarily choose a lender from the bank you are happy with and that you just set up your free small business account with. Maybe the best lender for you works at a competing bank and will work harder for you in the hopes of someday getting your deposits.

You will want to interview at least ten different loan officers at ten different banks. If you are just starting out, here is a sample script you can use to get started. When you call your bank, ask to speak with a commercial lending officer, and begin:

> "I am looking into some investment real estate options, and wondered if you could tell me about some of your different programs."

Right now, you are on a fact-finding mission. Take notes. Dedicate a notepad to these conversations with the ten loan officers you interview. List each loan officer on a separate page, and ask the following questions of each:

- What type of commercial investments does your bank specialize in?
- Do you hold your own loans or do you sell them?
- What are your commercial rates right now?
- What percentage of the transaction price do you keep at close? (also known as "points" or "fees")
- How much time do you require to close a transaction?

- How long does it take to close? If we started today, when would you expect to have funds to escrow?
- What paperwork do you need to see to get a loan (property) pre-approved?
- How much of a down payment do you require for an established mobile home park?

Your loan officer is going to become one of your best friends. Choose someone professional with whom you have a great rapport and who shows genuine interest in your future.

Your new loan officer will want to see you succeed, because that is a great reflection on his or her good judgment bringing you into their portfolio. They are also looking for you to bring in lots of repeat business, so they will do everything in their power to make the numbers work for you and ensure your present and future success, on this deal and on future deals which they hope you will do with them.

Next, find a realtor who has experience transacting commercial real estate. Ideally, this person has experience in mobile home park sales, but such experience is not necessary; they will learn along side you as you start writing and submitting offers on parks. You are going to want to include specific language and contingencies in your offer to purchase a park, so it is important to find someone who is comfortable including your list of whims. You want a broker who is working for and representing your best interest. Your realtor is often the only contact the sellers and their selling broker have with your company. Find someone to represent you who presents themselves well and respects the seriousness of the profession. Realtors have a lot at stake in getting the deal done correctly. It is up to you if your sellers ever meet you. You can be an anonymous buyer and handle everything through your broker, lawyer, and title company.

I also recommend you find yourself a very reliable person or team to help you with repairs, or to help you assess repairs quickly before calling a licensed repair person. This person might be your spouse, a family member, or even yourself. There may come a time when you need help with repairs if you are too busy, or traveling. When you queue your team ahead of time, you will avoid costly last-minute hires should you encounter a time-sensitive repair, such as someone driving a semi-truck through your park and smashing a park water main.

You may also wish to confide in a professional adviser. This person is the one you trust the most and can bounce all your crazy, wild, hair-brained ideas off. Most likely, this person will be a spouse, child, parent, or trusted friend who has an interest for business and does not compete with you. This needs to be the person who wants you to be successful and happy no matter what. This person will tell you when you are taking on too much or when it just plain sounds undoable. Choose someone whose opinion you respect and who has your best interest at heart.

I cannot overemphasize the value of a good tax accountant. I hear arguments against this all the time because of the expense. A good tax accountant is invaluable. The tax laws are like ever-shifting sands, and you are guaranteed to miss the latest nuances if you are self-preparing. When he or she is not doing taxes, your accountant is likely at classes studying how to prepare your taxes under all the new regulations come next tax season.

Finally, I would encourage you to network with other park owners. You will enjoy exchanging ideas and hearing about different scenarios they have encountered in their communities. They will be especially helpful with connecting you to resources that have served them well in your state or surrounding area.

CHAPTER NINE
BUYING VERSUS DEVELOPING

When you are researching your park, do not be lured in by the little catch phrase "room for expansion" or "plenty of room for development." All of a sudden, you envision your park doubling or tripling in size, all for the affordable price of one small mobile home park!

If it was that easy and that profitable to develop, are not you wondering why the sellers have not already done so? The reality is, although not impossible, that it is incredibly difficult and expensive to expand a park.

If you own an older park, which many are, you may actually jeopardize your investment, and risk *losing* your entire park if you step outside your grandfather status which may allow your present park to exist as-is inside the city limits.

Change your grandfather status and you change everything. Developing is not unattainable, it is just not anything I would encourage a first-time park buyer to tackle.

Expansion is expensive and challenging. Even after you have navigated the questions of city council and been approved by all your neighbors for expansion, then comes the part you never hear about: the city's very own systems' development charges (SDC's).

Each city sets its own SDC's, and depending on how amenable your city is to growth, these may or may not be affordable. In some cities, these fees cost hundreds of thousands of dollars before you even stick a shovel in the ground and start paying for the actual cost of your development.

You want to purchase a "turn-key" park. You want to know what you are getting when you buy. If it says 20 spaces, you are dealing with 20 spaces. Ensure all spaces are in good working order when you close, and you will have a nice 20-space park.

Be very careful to purchase a park that is already fully operational. You want to know exactly what you are getting into. There will be enough other surprises without one of them being your space count.

CHAPTER TEN
QUESTIONS BEFORE
BUYING A PARK

You will want to ask a very detailed list of questions before even considering buying a property. You should fill out a new sheet of these questions for each park you study. I print out these answers and put them in a file with all the information I collect on each individual park. This will keep your decision more organized when you are ready to compare all the parks you have looked at.

- [ ] What is the contact information for the sellers or sellers' listing broker?
- [ ] What is the name of the sellers?
- [ ] What is the sellers' or their listing broker's phone number?
- [ ] What is the name of the mobile home park?
- [ ] What is the price of the mobile home park?
- [ ] What is the park's address?
- [ ] How many developed, legal, fully operational spaces are in the park?
- [ ] What are the space rents?

- ☐ What are physically in the trailer spaces? Are there manufactured homes, recreational vehicles, travel trailers, or permanent rv's in the spaces?
- ☐ Does the park accept overnighters and are there any overnight tenants presently in the park?
- ☐ Does the park facilities include public restrooms and showers?
- ☐ Is there a laundry facility located inside the park? If so, is this facility open to the public? How much income is this bringing in? Who has the keys to the coin-operated machines and is collecting those coins each month? Does the park own the washers and dryers or are they leased?
- ☐ Are there water and sewer maps for the mobile home park?
- ☐ How many vacancies does the park presently have? Why are there vacancies?
- ☐ What is the age of the park?
- ☐ When was the park plumbing last updated?
- ☐ What is the age of the electrical boxes for the trailer hook-ups?
- ☐ What kind of plumbing is in the ground for the park water supply?

- ☐ Have the sellers had any maintenance concerns with the water lines?
- ☐ Have the sellers had any repairs or issues with the sewer lines?
- ☐ What is the age of the electrical systems? What have the problems been with these?
- ☐ What amperage are the electrical hook-ups and are they adequate for servicing present and future tenants' amperage requirements?
- ☐ Is the mobile home park on city water or on its own well? If on a well, who tests the water? How frequently does the county require the well water to be tested? What are the scheduled tests for this county and how much do they cost?
- ☐ Is the mobile home park on city sewer or on its own septic system? If septic, what is the age and configuration of the drain fields?
- ☐ Who pays the electric bill?
- ☐ Who pays the trash? What type of disposal is in place? Does this park utilize individual trash can service or is there a centralized dumpster?
- ☐ What are the bills the park pays each month?
- ☐ Are all the spaces in good working order? If not, why?
- ☐ Is the park gravel, paved, or a mixture of both?

☐ Does the park have a history of tree roots in the plumbing and sewer systems?

☐ How many acres comprise this park property?

☐ Who maintains the mobile home park, including lawn care and leaf disposal?

☐ Is there an on-site manager? What is his or her arrangement or compensation?

☐ Why are the sellers selling?

☐ Are there any bills paid by the park in addition to the monthly expenses?

☐ What are the property taxes? (this amount should never exceed one month's rent or else your rents are too low or your taxes are too high)

☐ Is there any room for expansion? How does your county feel about expansion? Have the sellers ever inquired about expanding the park?

☐ Is the park considered conforming or non-conforming use, or is it grandfathered in?

☐ Who are the park's neighbors? Who is around the park? (you want a well-serviced area with lots of stores, fast food, gas stations, services, and big box stores)

☐ What is the designation of the park: family, all ages, 55 and older, 62 and older? If the park claims a discrimination (i.e. 55 and older park means they discriminate against tenants younger than age 55), exactly what percentage of the park is in that age distinction? Is there proof with the state that the park is allowed that designation?

☐ Where do the renters work? What do they do?

☐ What is the industry surrounding the park?

☐ With whom is the park insured? Has the park had any claims in the last two years? If so, what were the claims for and by whom?

☐ Is anyone presently being sued? Why?

☐ Is everybody current on his or her rent payment? If not, who and why?

☐ Are there any known problems in the mobile home park?

☐ What is the next thing the sellers' would fix in the mobile home park?

☐ Have there been any evictions in the last two years for drugs or crime in the park?

☐ How do the tenants pay the rent each month?

☐ Is there anything else you should know about this property?

For a more-comprehensive list of questions to ask before you purchase your mobile home park, please see our Form Supplemental Due Diligence on www.MobileHomeParkInfo.com and click Forms.

CHAPTER ELEVEN
WHY ARE THEY SELLING?
What Can You Fix That Will Make This Park Profitable?

Why is the seller selling? Are they parting with an unprofitable park? Why is it unprofitable?

Very rarely do families sell profitable mobile home parks, unless they just want the money, or if the sellers are elderly and wanting to retire off the proceeds from the sale of the park.

How can mobile home parks be considered real moneymakers, yet there are so many on the market that are losing thousands of dollars each month? Why are some of these parks so successful, and some so upside-down? The answers lie in getting some honest dialogue as to why the sellers are selling.

Perk up your antenna. They will drop clues, and you need to listen for anything at all that strikes you as incongruous, or inconsistent with what you have been lead to believe about the property or its history.

Some sellers are very elderly and wishing to retire, and they either have no children, or no children interested in the park. Their kids would rather have the money.

Other older sellers will want to sell to you on contract, because they are looking for a steady and reliable source of income into their retirement, without what has become the inconvenience of running their own park. They are willing to carry a sales contract in exchange for steady monthly payments and a little bit of interest, which will save both parties costly refinancing or new financing costs if handled through a title company.

You will encounter parks that are being sold by trusts and estates. These are properties placed in holding trusts for the children who have no interest in learning how to manage a park. The heirs wish to claim their inheritance immediately by selling, instead of capturing a lifetime of cash flow from holding the park in trust.

The sellers you need to interview most diligently are the younger sellers. They will unfurl some of the most interesting problems, many of which can be fixed by you. Just make your offer knowing it is a disadvantaged property.

Implement your ideas after you close, do not telegraph them ahead of time. The sellers have had all these years to figure out they should combine dumpsters into one six-yard and pay half the trash bill they are currently paying. Do not let them benefit from your due diligence. It could quickly backfire on you like it has done me, and they will use your fresh researched ideas to keep their park and make the profits themselves.

Younger sellers are particularly interesting because they typically have owned only one park, and it is the park they are selling. You are buying what used to be *their* dream. They are often angry at life, angry at themselves, and especially hateful of the property they are trying to unload.

The reasons I have heard why younger folks are selling include:

- we are getting a divorce (translated: because of the stupid park)
- I bought another business (because this one is vacuuming all the money out of my wallet)
- it is just too far to drive (right....*you* are supposed to drive six hours to manage this property, but one hour is too far for the sellers?)

It is only upon closer scrutiny that you peel back the real reason these sellers on are the off-ramp.

The folks getting a divorce were losing thousands each month to an on-site manager charging them $2000 to mow the grass. The wife was the bookkeeper, so at least she knew she was going to pocket $500 each month. The husband was the guy working another job to keep the park bills paid and footing the bill for everybody else. Their manager also received free rent, free utilities, free firewood, and was parking about a dozen friends there for free, paying him under the table, tenants who did not show up on the books, but who were all hooked up to park utilities.

Upon closer inspection of the park where the seller "had bought another business," his water bills at the park he was selling actually exceeded his monthly rents! He was subsidizing his own park with another job he was working as well. He was also entangled with partners who had silently invested, which he thought was a great idea at one time. But after several years, the partner was still collecting profits much like franchise fees, but the working partner was not making a dime! According to their arrangement, he was spending hours each month hassling no-pays. He had to get out to preserve his sanity!

And finally, the seller who did not feel like driving one hour each month to visit his park, had a very interesting situation: a railroad ran through it, and a welding shop operated beside it, and a freeway bordered the other side. This little park should never have been built. It was dusty, it was noisy through no fault of its own, and it was sliding down a dirty hill.

Another scenario you may encounter is partnerships gone sour. There are many of these situations, where the partners are forced into selling. Partnerships are rarely equitable in my opinion.

Avoid partnerships at all costs. Just don't partner with anyone if you can absolutely avoid it.

Obviously, if your sellers are bitter partners, then someone had to partner because they could not do it on their own. After time, this disparate arrangement breeds resentment, usually from the person running the park, doing all the work and feeling like they are taking arrows on the front line, resenting the other partner who sits in a cool office or plays tennis on indoor cooled courts, oblivious to the other's pain.

Partnerships breaking up are very interesting situations for you as a buyer. People in these situations have hounded me, begging me to please buy their park. Disgruntled partners have offered me zero down in exchange for please just taking over the property and getting them out of the picture. Unhappy partnerships may offer to carry, or propose any number of creative structures for you to purchase, whatever it takes to get their name off the property.

You still need to vet and critically analyze any property. Just because it is easy to get into, this may not be the best park for you and you will want to be just as thorough with your analysis and due diligence of making sure your park checks out, even if the sellers are offering you a zero down scenario. This may not be a park you decide to purchase.

Unfortunately, some sellers are unethical and have committed fraud or are intending to defraud you. Fraud is a difficult situation because it is time consuming and expensive to prove, and some sellers may get away with it at your expense. It is best to have purchased your park through your LLC, have a good business lawyer to advise you, and maintain good park business insurance policy in case you ever encounter a fraud situation.

The absolute bottom line of why anyone is selling a park, regardless of what description from above they might fit, is because the park is a hassle to run and someone is not making buckets of money.

Very few sellers sell a profitable park unless they just need their money now and stand to make a large profit from the park sale. If a park is making money, someone somewhere in the seller's family is hanging onto it. This means you are likely buying problems, so that is just something to be aware of going in.

The key is to figuring out before you purchase, what and how you can fix the issues you've identified, to turn your park profitable! Here is a handy reference guide to troubleshoot whatever reason your sellers are selling you their park, issues your potential park might be having, and what you can reasonably do to fix them:

PROBLEMS AND SOLUTIONS:

UTILITY ISSUES:

- **Water Bill Too High:**
solution Contact your local city to find out how the water is billed. Is it a flat rate / flat rate + consumption / or straight usage charges? If the city is billing off straight consumption (i.e. one unit of water used times a set price), inquire about installing meters to each home. The city will likely be able to work you up a quote for this service. If the city installs your water meters, see if they will also read them. If your city is not interested or too expensive to enact individual meters (the last city I

check with wanted $5,100 per meter they installed), then get bids from local contractors to have these installed. If their bids are a big number, consider having your broker add an addendum to your purchase agreement under one of your contingency provisions that the water meter install be offset at close. Once you have your meters installed, or if you have a date of completion on the horizon, issue a three-month utility pass through notice to your tenants that you will be charging them for their individual water usage. You can then recoup this entire bill from your tenants.

- **Sewer Bill Too High:**

solution Is the sewer bill part of the water bill? If the sewer charges equal the monthly water usage multiplied by the sewer rate, find out from your city about individual meters to each unit. Either the city can provide this service, or you can hire someone to install these individually. If you have meters installed, these will need to be read each month. You will need to issue a three-month utility pass-through notice to your tenants, then start passing along their individual expenses from their meter. If your sewer bill comes from a separate provider, add it to your water bill and divide by the number of units in your park to find out what each is costing you per month. If you feel it is necessary, consider a rent raise to cover these two critical utilities.

- **Electric Bill Too High:**

solution Find out from your broker exactly what the electric bill is paying. Is it common area lights? Is it the laundry / shop / office / storage? Those bills should only run you about $50 or $60 per month, for a park of up to about four acres. You should never be on the hook for tenant electricity. If you are, there is something wrong. Inquire about individual meters to your local electric company. If these are already in place but you are being billed on a common park meter, issue a three month utility pass-through notice to your tenants, and read or have these electric meters read every single month and bill your tenants for this utility.

- **Trash Bill Too High:**

solution Garbage companies are fun to work with. You actually talk to people who have a finite number of products and services available to your park, and they are always happy to discuss these with you, the customer. Take about 10 or 15 minutes and interview every single provider that will consider service to your park. Garbage companies have territories, and you might find that there is only one that will provide service to your area. That is okay. They will still have an assortment of products for you to choose from. Your options will include can versus dumpster, and then vary on the size of dumpster and number of pickups. Ask what they recommend for your size park. They determine this based on your tenant count and number bags will fit inside a dumpster, and they will size accordingly. Inquire about every option. Maybe a smaller dumpster emptied every week is more economical than a larger dumpster emptied every other week. This is all money you get to keep, so negotiate the best scenario. Do not be sentimental about keeping can service just because the park "has always done it that way." Do what makes sense for your new budget, and go the most affordable route on the garbage.

If recycling is not required for your area, then you will want to be careful since this is an area that garbage companies get rich at your expense. I once discovered that we were being billed and extra $25 per can on top of our regular bill, because the tenants refused to sort their recycling and used their recycle bin as an extra garbage can. The recycle bill, which should have been free, was costing me an extra $475 per month on top of a $270 garbage bill since the tenants refused to sort their trash. In the end, I pulled the recycling and yard debris carts since they were being abused.

Other parks will be conscientious and ask for recycling, which should not cost your park anything. But you will just want to watch your bill if you add this service.

- **Insurance Bill Too High:**

solution Before you even buy your park, I want you to start shopping for commercial coverage. Insurance is such a critical bill, you really need to nail this expense down before you start crunching your numbers. Shop every single insurance company you can find in your state that covers mobile home parks. Tell them what you are considering, and have them quote apples to apples so you can compare.

One of the biggest bills you see on profit and loss statements when you are analyzing parks is their bill for insurance. It is usually between $3,000 to

$7,000 per year. I overpaid my insurance for years, too. I stayed on with the insurance carrier that came with my first park. It was not until the attacks on the Twin Towers, when I got an additional bill requiring terrorist insurance on all my properties, that I got suspicious and started shopping around. What a surprise, that instead of $3,700 per year that my insurance should have been closer to $500 per year!

Shop this expense until you have no more options. You have to have affordable insurance coverage; this is one bill you will have the rest of the time you own the park.

- **Cable Bill Too High:**
solution Why is this park providing cable to its residents? Cable is a big red-flag expense because it is an elective utility. Most often, those who feel they need cable find a way to get it. If you are going to lose a pile of renters if you shut off cable, see if you can renegotiate with the service provider. You have a big negotiating tool: your entire park! Let the cable company know they are going to lose your business if they cannot reconfigure your bill. You might also consider only raising the rent on

those who choose to hook up to cable, so you can recapture the bill that way.

MAINTENANCE ISSUES:

- **Yard Care Too High:**

solution Is the park's current groundskeeper paid monthly to mow and maintain the landscape? If you are unhappy with how much lawn care is costing the park, request all service contracts terminate at time of close and stipulate you will renegotiate those. When I first bought several of my parks, I came around every several weeks and did my own grounds-keeping. This got me on site so tenants could see me involved, and they had a chance to visit with me about their concerns. Later, when my schedule got too hectic to get around to keep up my properties, I bid out the work to several tenants on site who owned their own lawn-care businesses. We discussed service level and agreed upon a monthly rate of $160, which I had the tenant deduct from his rent. On another park, the tenant pays his rent in full and is reimbursed $100 out of petty cash. Watch this number when you purchase your park. You will be paying this bill every single month, it needs to be something you can afford. A park I looked at recently that was losing thousands of dollars each year is still paying their lawn care service $1,100 per month to mow five little postage stamp lawns. Look at every line item when you purchase, even one as insignificant as grounds upkeep. The devil is in the little details; you need to scrutinize every line item that costs you money.

- **Tons Of Repairs:**

solution Ask to review receipts as part of your due diligence to find out what your sellers are claiming as repairs. There could be a huge electric bill to split out meters, which would be a non-recurring charge; there could be a large bill for resurfacing the blacktop, which you would not incur again for ten or fifteen years. If the repair bills are steady and outrageous, find out what they are constantly fixing. Are the sewer pipes made out of orangeburg? Are the water lines made up of copper, galvanized, garden hoses, and Band-Aids? Assess what is being repaired and figure out if you will have that same bill. Likely you will not. Many repairs you can take care of yourself, and you can get yourself an assistant by hiring a local handyman for about $15 per hour. This can be negotiated. I pay $25 per hour because my handyman responds quickly when I have emergency repairs. If the repair is serious and will be very costly down the road, such as broken roof trusses over a pool, or defective service hookups, have your broker renegotiate an addendum to your purchase agreement that the repairs must be completed by the seller, or compensated for, in order for you to close the transaction.

- **Deferred Maintenance or Infrastructure Repairs:**

solution: You will want to have the sellers identify and show you receipts and work orders for proof that they have stayed current on any infrastructure maintenance. Infrastructure is any system in the park that supports the habitability of the tenants, such as electrical systems to each space, water pipes, and sewer systems. These repairs could include updates to code or fire safety, for example of the electrical boxes were built in the 1960s or earlier. You will want to see proof of all updates to make sure the water lines and sewer lines will last you another 40 or 50 years. There are a number of plumbing and rooter services that will inexpensively scope and camera the entire park systems underground for you and provide you with a cd for viewing on your computer. You can also hire several inspectors to help you with the due diligence process when you are examining your park. Another way to double check on park infrastructure is to contact the county or city office that would have been responsible for issuing any repair permits, and check the past history of the park for repairs. If the sellers are telling you work was recently completed, but you cannot verify this, then perhaps the work was completed without proper permits. It is also a good idea to have a number of contractors come out to look at the systems to give you bids for what they see might need attention. This will get you the best picture since the contractor will likely bid any projects for free, and you can use these bids to negotiate a lower price based on the actual condition of the park, lowered by the amounts you might have to pay out for future repairs and updates. For example, if you identify a number of issues with the blacktop parking lot, and have a bid for resurfacing at $26,000, you can use this bid to lower the amount you decide to offer for the property, since you will not be offering full price once you discover things that might need your attention that the sellers did not maintain.

- **Restrooms:**

solution   If you have restrooms in your park that are costing you money every month for supplies, find out who is using these facilities. Are they for overnight guests? Research changing your park's designation to long-term or month-to-month tenants, so you do not need to provide restrooms for your clientele. If you are not mandated to provide restrooms for your park, lock them.

- **Laundry:**

solution   Why would laundry ever cost a park more than it makes? If you have an unprofitable laundromat on your park, you need to close it. Do not be sentimental about losing money. Your laundromat should at least pay its own water, electric, and gas bills. Find out from your operator who you lease the machines from, or from a local handyman if you own your own machines, how to increase the rate. Your laundromat needs to at least cover its own bills, and leave a couple hundred a month on the table for your petty cash repair fund and gas for your lawn mowers.

MANAGEMENT ISSUES:

- **Manager Being Paid More Than The Park Is Making:**

solution Stipulate at time of close that all service contracts terminate with the sale. This is the best time and easiest way to fire a bad manager. They sunk the previous owners, you sure do not need that manager's help.

- **Office / Phone Charges:**

solution Never pay anyone's phone bill. You are likely looking at bills for an office phone. Just give your new tenants your phone number. You are not going to be staffing an on-site office.

You are likely not retaining the park manager. Even if you choose to keep the manager, so many people have their own cell phones. Just let them know if they wish to remain in that position, the new owners are not providing a phone. If they do not have free long distance on their cell, offer to purchase them a calling card, which you can get at many box stores for about $20. If you trust this individual enough to be running your park, they are likely collecting the laundry proceeds for you. Have them take money for stamps or paper out of the petty cash and provide you a receipt. You should not have big supplies bills for a park office. This should never run more than about $10 per month for office supplies. If so, examine where your money is going.

- **Advertising Expenses Are Too High:**
solution There are many affordable ways to advertise. I devote Chapter 24 to different advertising ideas that are free or nearly free. This should not be a big expense for you.

- **Payroll Taxes / Expenses:**
solution This is not a bill you should have. Why are there payroll taxes? If you run your park yourself, you are an owner/operator and do not pay payroll taxes on yourself. If you retain a manager, most places base compensation on a commissioned basis. This means you might be sending a 1099 at the end of the year from your accountant, but you are not running your park as a stand-alone business. You are renting spaces, not running a company out of your park. If there is any dispute over this, ask your broker to stipulate that all service contracts between the park and employees terminate at time

of close. If you have any questions at all, call several property management companies in your area. You do not pay payroll to property managers. The easiest solution is to manage your own park.

- **Professional / Accounting Fees:**

solution You should control this expense yourself and pay the accountant of your own choosing. You know what this costs you each year, so scrutinize whatever the sellers are claiming in this field.

Often, accounting fees are where sellers hide whatever wages they are paying themselves. Buy your own software and keep your own books, then the only expense you will have is hiring a tax preparer.

ISSUES WITH CITY OR COUNTY: UNPAID SYSTEMS DEVELOPMENT CHARGES / ANY CARRY OVER IMPROVEMENTS TO CITY UTILITIES OR SIDEWALKS:

solution Any unpaid system's development charges (SDC's) or improvements that the seller is making payments to the city on (sewer upgrades, new sidewalks, new city trees, etc.) are not your problem. Have your broker write into your contingencies that these must be paid at close. You do not need any ancillary bills hanging over your park when you take over.

UNPAID BACK TAXES:

solution The sellers unpaid back taxes are actually not your problem or your responsibility. You will want to transact your purchase and your closing, when you take possession of your park, through escrow and through a title company. Through your broker or your attorney, whoever is drawing up the papers for your transaction, stipulate that all back taxes must be paid by your sellers, out of the sellers column, at close. This will also be a condition of your new lender, and you will likely be prepaying at least one year's taxes at close if you have financed through a traditional lender. Ask your closing officer at the title company to provide you proof the back taxes have been paid. You can also check with your county tax assessor after the transaction has been recorded if you need further proof or assurance these have been paid.

SELLER ISSUES:

- ### Partnership Dissolving:

solution Have your broker negotiate your offer so there are no holdover partners. You are starting clean with a fresh slate of players. You have no interest in retaining any aspect of a broken partnership.

- ### Loan Too Expensive:

solution Some sellers financed their park at unprofitable interest rates. This is very expensive money. You do not know what their situation was at the point of purchase. Come in with a new loan, your own financing, and always close through escrow and a bona fide title company. This way you are completely protected by title insurance and there are no holdover lenders or prevailing first or second liens on your property. You need to hold a clear title, with no funny loan clouds from the sellers.

- ### Interest Too High On Sellers' Loan:

solution Negotiate your own brand new loan and interest rate with your lender. The sellers may have purchased a property at a time when the market only offered high interest rates on properties of this category. They may have entered on favorable terms, then found themselves on an escalator arm that made their payment unmanageable.

TENANT ISSUES:

- **Too Many Vacancies / Park Empty:**
solution I have dedicated an entire chapter in this book (Chapter 24) to ideas to fill up your park. Make sure you are buying in a high-density area. Look for fast food franchises nearby or national franchise stores such as pharmacies and movie rental chains that likely conduct market research by counting the number of roofs in that given area. If you see any large national franchises near your park, you are likely buying in a high-density area and will easily be able to fill your park.

- **Problem Tenants: Drugs / Gangs / Violence:**
solution Evictions are part of mobile home park ownership. If you find a park that you think has

investment potential, do not let the current tenant population discourage you. You can go online to a mugshot site, or a criminal listing organization, such as the National Victim Notification Network or vinelink.com (Victim's Notification Every Day), and research if any of these tenants or guests have warrants pending. It is very easy to contact problem tenants' parole officers or law enforcement and request assistance and advice in cleaning up your park

- **Late Pays / No Pays And Rent Collection Issues:**

solution Be strict from the first second you assume management of your park. You are running a business with an obligation to your family, your lender, and your own commitments. You are not running a charity. If a tenant does not pay, they are stealing from you and everyone that counts on you. Collect from the tenant and contribute to the charity of your choosing. The seller's inability to collect past rents is not your problem. Insist that full rents be fully accounted for, prorated, and paid to you from the date of close (i.e. rents are due on the first: if you close on the 15th of the month, you are entitled to be paid half the month's rents. These rents are due to you at time of close). Do not accept an excuse of "the rents are still coming in" to account for rents being missing at close; this is not your problem. All rents must appear as accounted for in full, and prorated at close. Do not assume past word-of-mouth agreements between seller and tenant. You start fresh with brand new rental agreements for everyone. All rents are due on the first of the month, then you should issue a 72-hour notices on the eighth (refer to issuing notices Chapter 21).

There are several issues, that if you find these in a park, it would be best to just pass on that property and keep looking.

The first of these matters is anything environmental, such as a protected butterfly, or a soil issue such as arsenic. Environmental issues will marry your park to the Department of Environmental Quality (DEQ) and to their best friend, the Environmental Protection Agency (EPA). If you even hear them mentioned, you need to immediately pass on this park. Please do not even consider purchasing this park if it enjoys the constant company of DEQ and EPA.

These agencies are not your friend and will be in control of your permitting which is expensive. These permitting junctures allow the agencies to dictate modifications to your infrastructure, such as a drain field, and they may require you convert your entire property onto a new system, even if only several homes are affected. Plans for permits must be engineered and drafted by expensive experts, of whom your state may only have several, so you are now at the mercy of the experts and they are expensive.

Some DEQ permits are now "living" permits, such as for a septic drain field in the county, which is a clever way to extract thousands of dollars for fees annually for services you are now required to use, and you are now permanently under either monthly or quarterly sampling and review, and now yearly review, all at your expense since the park has to agree to this new arrangement just to keep the park doors open.

I believe this clouds your park if you decide to sell. And even if you sell the park and notify DEQ of the sale, it is not enough to relieve your responsibility in the eyes of DEQ. The process to transfer a living permit is very complicated and paper-work intensive, and you will be on the hook for a long time trying to navigate all the proper forms and to get them out of your life.

In my opinion, all these new environmental regulations are a back door approach to putting parks out of business through the disproportionate costs for permitting and repairs. These agencies require expensive systems which do not make good business sense when a simpler solution would work. But that is not a choice you are allowed to make when government agencies are designing your park systems.

The EPA does not play fair, aggressively targeting parks in my area for having one billionth of a particle over the allowable limit for arsenic in the drinking water. One billionth. To put this in perspective, there are 66 parts per billion arsenic in organic baby food; there are 25 parts per billion arsenic in most beer, amounts which doctors say are trace, what you are breathing in the air or already have in your hair, or the amounts found in organic breakfast or energy bars. What I am saying is the standard now enforced by the EPA has changed recently, and is now unreasonable and heavy-handed in my opinion.

But parks around me, and my park included, were subject to aggressive enforcement and hefty fines for being one billionth of a particle out of compliance. The solution, carbon treatment systems or conversions to local water, cost the parks cumulatively hundreds of thousands of dollars for no measurable benefit to the health of anyone.

If you suspect a property may have had or will have environmental concerns, you can request a Level One Environmental Study, known as a pre-purchase environmental site assessment, and ask more questions during this process. If the inspector identifies areas of concern with the underlying soils or structures on the property, he or she will recommend you move to a Phase Two site assessment survey, at which point you will be certain that this is not the park you are going to be pursuing or consider purchasing.

There are too many clean and healthy parks to get involved with some other sellers mess they are now trying to sell to you, which could include old tanks, dumping chemicals from an old dry cleaners, or a failed meth lab. You do not ever want environmental clean up issues, and most parks do not have any issues; so it is best to find a healthy, profitable, turn-key park.

Another situation to just avoid entirely is any park or area that is subject to rent control. Other names for this are rent stabilization, and rent fixing. This is the result of public pressure. You absolutely ***cannot*** own and run a park where rent control is practiced. To buy a mobile home park in a rent stabilized area is not an investment, it is financial suicide. These areas to avoid include over 100 cities and counties in California, parts of New York, Washington D.C., New Jersey, Boston, and Cambridge, and in some parts of Canada.

Rent fixing reduces the park owner to a non-profit charity where it is no longer rational or advantageous to own a park. This is common sense, since the utilities, and park expenses, and taxes go up, expenses which the owner is responsible for by law to provide habitability. But the park owner has no control over these expenses. To not allow park owners control over rent increases, to even proportionately raise the rents to even keep the park from going bankrupt, will drive parks out of business.

In California, the results have been devastating. Since rent controls began, there have been no new parks built in the last 22 years. That is an outrage. Next, park owners started going out of business and simply took their rentals off the market to keep from going bankrupt.

The California judges have continued to favor public outcry, and another case was just awarded to tenants in favor of rent stabilization in early June that is said to affect hundreds of thousands of renters in parks across the state of California.

Rent fixing legislation is cumbersome. The laws are punitive on park owners, and complicated, with very few lawyers even able to understand. This is not fair to park owners who serve such an important role in the availability of affordable safe housing.

You will also want to make sure the property taxes on the park do not exceed one months take home rents on the property. This is a good ratio. But you will see some parks, for example in areas of New York, where the rents exceed three or four months of all rents collected. Such taxation situations are not conducive to running a park as an investment. You would be serving as a tax collector for those three or four months, and trying to keep up with your mortgage, and the rest of the park bills. High property taxes are just not worth it. You are not a tax collector, you are an investor. And disproportionate property tax rates are out of your control and need to be avoided. Again, there are too many good parks whose taxes are a fraction of one month's rents which will provide you a nice return on your investment.

So in conclusion, you will want to avoid parks with any environmental red flags, or in areas subject to rent control, or in areas that take a third of your rents for the year to pay property taxes – all matters that are simply out of your control and must be completely avoided.

Otherwise, the good news is, that you can fix almost any other issue facing a park that is causing the seller to sell the property. You will want to spend some time with your sellers or their broker, finding out why the sellers are *really* selling their dream, so it will not become your nightmare! If you check what they tell you against the solutions earlier in this chapter, you will quickly see if you can reasonably effect a solution to make their problem park, a highly profitable park for you!

CHAPTER TWELVE
CONGRATULATIONS!
You Bought A Park!

Congratulations! After much research, due diligence, and negotiation, your mobile home park transaction is headed to escrow which is the title company where you will "close" the transaction and take ownership and possession of your new mobile home park investment.

Several days before you sign and close at the title company, some very important things need to happen. Contact your local branch of your state's mobile housing community. Purchase forms you think you will need, such as 72-hour notices, 30-day notices, and month-to-month lease agreements for your new tenants.

You will need to prepare brand new leases for all your new tenants. You need to meet each tenant and get the new leases signed immediately. This is the legal basis upon which all your transactions are based. This gives you the legal ability to collect rent.

There are several key documents you need to get into the hands of your tenants as soon as possible:

- Introductory letter from you with your contact information
- Letter of policy from your park (your state ordinances which you can find online for most states will have very specific language and details you need to put in your letter of policy)
- Space dimensions for each space
- A copy of your park rules
- New lease or month-to-month rental agreement, which your new tenant needs to sign. Give each his or her own copy of this new agreement.
- Arbitration agreement

Have your tenants already set up in whatever software you will be using to track and record your rents.

You also need to have all rents prorated at close. This means that if you sign and take ownership of the park in the middle of the month, half that month's rental income is yours. The sellers have an obligation to give you all the rent they have collected for your pro-ration of ownership. What if they have not collected all the rents? This is not your problem. Insist that the title officer prorate as though the rents came in complete.

You cannot assume or collect bad debts owed the sellers. Those are gone unless the sellers had the tenant sign a separate promissory note. This is not anything you want to get involved in. Be aware of the tenants they are having issues with, but you are starting with a clean slate.

It is important you know which tenants are not current, but you have no legal basis to collect the seller's bad debts.

Next, there needs to be a termination of all service and employment contracts with your parks that the sellers may have contracted. These could include a groundskeeper, a linen or paper goods company, or a vending machine vendor. You have the right to renegotiate your own contracts and hire your own vendors if you choose. You are going to be running things a little differently. Choose carefully which services make sense to keep in your budget.

If you no longer wish a utility to be billed to the park, the sellers will need to contact the service provider to let them know there has been a change in ownership. It is important the sellers discontinue service at that time. If the sellers do not turn off a utility and it continues to be billed to them, but you are the one now getting the bill, it is not your obligation to pay. You did not contract the service. Contact the provider immediately and let them know. You need to send the bill to the sellers. They need to pay that charge pro-rated through the time of close, after which time there should be no more bills from that provider.

Usually, all bills come in the name of the sellers or their company. On the odd chance you get a bill that is addressed to the park, and it is a service provider you intend to keep, switch that bill into your company name and have it come to your P.O. Box so it does not get lost at your park and ultimately reflect on your credit.

Within the first few days of owning your park, contact all the utility companies you intend to keep in your park. Switch those providers into the name of your LLC.

This is going to be the easiest month of your park ownership. Your rents are already collected for the month, so relax for the rest of this month!

CHAPTER THIRTEEN
MANAGEMENT
Who Is Going To Manage Your Park For You?

Bad managers rank among the top two reasons people sell their mobile home parks, almost tied with out-of-control utilities and water/sewer bills. When you are looking for a mobile home park, the number one question you need to ask yourself - more important than how much is this going to cost me and how much is it going to make – is *who* is going to manage your mobile home park for you?

Asking you who is going to manage your park for you is really a trick question. The best answer is: *you* are going to manage your own mobile home park. You are buying a park that is not operating at top performance, or obviously it would not be for sale for such a good price to you. The last thing you should consider is keeping the current management in place. If it is an unprofitable park, the current management will sink you as fast as they are sinking the current owner. If the in-place manager had the interest or ability to fix what is wrong with your park, it would have been done by now!

Be wary of park deals where the owners are selling so much more than their park. They are selling a disadvantaged situation with a strong-arm manager who is earning more than the sellers are. The owners are selling because they are going broke, but they have made a manager very rich.

It is common to see on-site managers who enjoy free rent, free utilities, free firewood, free parking for multiple vehicles, free storage, free telephone and fax and long distance, free office supplies; in addition, they are often collecting a large percentage of the rents collected, they are keeping late fees they collect, and they are getting paid bonuses. And there is more. Most managers also charge by the hour for any handiwork, mowing, or grounds upkeep they do in addition to the rent collection duties.

A bad manager is a bad manager, no matter who employs him or her. Are there good managers? Absolutely. If you find a jewel, you are the luckiest buyer in the world.

There is no limit to the creative ways a bad manager can legally and creatively steal from you through his or her bookkeeping. Accounting cases are tough to prove and win because the managers often claim you benefited from repairs, and you are on the hook for those expenditures.

Would you trust someone you barely know with $2,000 every month? There are probably even members of your immediate family that you would not trust to hand you every penny of $2,000 cash every single month. You are talking some big numbers. This is a lot of money to most people, especially the demographic that may inhabit your park.

How about $6,000? Are you going to hand $6,000 in cash rents to your manger each month? How about $19,000? Per month, every single month, for years? Realistically, can *you* cover the mortgage and a month's worth of expenditures and utility bills out of your own pocket, out of your own savings, out of your family's grocery money, if a manager steals all your rents?

What if your manager is not completely happy with the amount you are paying him or her? What if this manager has checked around, and all the other managers in your area are getting paid 15 percent to do what he or she is doing for 10 percent? All the other managers are getting free rent, gas money, and a phone and fax machine in their home office. This manager is not. Just that little bit of unhappiness is going to irk someone who has to hand of thousands and thousands of dollars to you every month. Maybe this on-site manager is unhappy thinking about you getting all that income after he or she did all the work. Many rents are paid in cash to an on-site manager, raising the temptation to siphon off a little here and there without you ever knowing.

It is so easy for *you* to run your own mobile home parks and bypass what an on-site manager would do for you in your park. In Chapter 15, you will learn how little time is required each month for the nuts and bolts of running a park. Depending on the size of your park if you find a 4-space park up to a 400-space park, would you do one hour of book-work for a property bringing in anywhere from $2,000, to $19,000, to $160,000 gross income per month? Every single month? Even $2,000 is a lot of money to most people, especially to a lot of managers who might live onsite in a trailer while you are traveling on your yacht. Most park investors starting out try to find that hour or couple hours needed, or simply "hire" themselves as their own manager, thus creating a job for themselves and scaling back or quitting a day job.

Even if you have someone you completely trust collecting rents for you, I want you to consider one more reason why you should consider managing your own park: exposure. If your manager, who is your personal representative, makes a comment that is construed as discriminatory, you are facing fair housing accusations and you are going to court. The very least I have heard it costs to retain a fair housing attorney is in the ballpark of $50,000. This simply from your manager saying something along the lines of, "Maybe you want to park over here, in the kid-free section." Discrimination. You or your park manager are absolutely not allowed to discriminate. What if your manager tells a couple they will be comfortable in your park because there are no people of any other particular ethnicity? Discrimination. What if your manager annoys someone or botches a notice or an eviction? You are liable for their ignorance and incompetence.

You have worked so hard and so diligently to get into your first park. I want you to strongly consider running this park yourself. You are going to collect your own rents and pay your own bills and take your own phone calls from tenants.

It is worrisome and potentially stressful to turn that aspect of park ownership over to an individual who may not protect your best interest and who may endanger what you have worked so hard for. It is not worth the risk and liability of letting someone else you barely know or should not trust manage your park for you.

What if that individual is licensed and certified as a property management agency? In cases where two different managers stole thousands from me, they both had licenses and were current on all state requirements. These professional managers were still crooked, and although they did not know each other, both ultimately declared bankruptcy to avoid jail and repaying the in-excess of $37,000 that they had stolen over time from my properties.

Are there large park management companies, such as an arm of a local real estate brokerage, who are reputable, licensed, and capable of overseeing your park property? Absolutely, and I have hired several of these myself; my experience is that their fees are costly and make the most sense if you have a much-larger park to manage, such as 150+ spaces. Then the fees are prorated over the number of spaces, since fee schedules start with a flat ceiling: i.e. maybe their base rate is $1,500 to even consider managing your park, and then they may use a scale, for example additional fee per space, which is built into your monthly bill. Does this make sense for a small 20-space park that is only grossing about $10,000 to $12,000 in rents each month? That is your decision. These larger agencies also make money from fees for anything extra you need done: filling a vacancy, reading your park meters, and they will offer to pay all the park bills for you as well. Should you choose hire a large company to manage, at some point you will find yourself managing your manager and asking things like, why it takes four to six months to screen and re-rent a vacancy. They will be charging you to advertise the vacancy, but unbeknownst to you, you might very well be attracting renters for ALL the vacancies in that manager's profile. The tenant might just be offered and choose a space in one of their other parks with you never being the wiser.

In the beginning, regardless if you decide to delegate management to a professional third party down the road, you will want to manage your own park.

CHAPTER FOURTEEN
TIME-SAVING SOFTWARE

In order to maximize your time, you will want to invest in a rental management software program. Depending on your area, a trip to your local electronics box store should offer quite a few options for rental management software. Even the most basic program will get you started managing your property. The one I started with cost $99.

You want to look for property management software that will allow you to enter rents for as many units as you purchase. Good software, even the most basic, is able to generate your tax reports in a single click; this feature alone makes it worth the price. If you prefer to generate your own spreadsheet in lieu of purchasing software, you will want to enter rent collections and itemize expenditures. Tax time may be cumbersome for you if you choose to design your own spreadsheet program. The rental property management software has report-generating features built-in, and assimilates your tax reports for you.

Many of the older parks you look at will still be keeping rent rolls by handwritten accounting. This method worked for years and still works, but it is very time consuming and come tax time you still have to calculate all your expenses and enter everything on your software in order to generate your tax reports.

You need your software program to track rents, enter expenses, and tabulate quarterly and yearly reports. You also need to be able to create an invoice and a statement. Most programs will allow you to generate a receipt of payment. This is unnecessary unless you are accepting cash, in which case you should be using a duplicate receipt book and writing them a receipt on the spot.

I have used Quicken Rental Property Manager in my office, and I also run the latest version of Quickbooks Pro. Neither is tooled to the specifics of park management, but both programs will save you a lot of time.

You should consider running the back-up system for your primary rent roll tracker because you may need to generate invoices and statements, depending on how you set up your rent collection system, which I will detail in Chapter 20. For the sole purpose of creating invoices and statements, I back up the rent manager with Quickbooks Pro.

When you purchase your software, be sure to keep immediate and accurate records of your rent collection and expenditures. Enter each renter on a separate line, along with as much information you can about that tenant for your own records.

CHAPTER FIFTEEN
GO AWAY
And Still Manage Your Own Park

There are some important techniques you can employ to turn your park into a well-oiled machine. Most importantly, you need access to the Internet. If you are not yet using online banking, please get familiar with your bank's web site. Remote banking will be such a time saver for you. The secret to passive income is you want it to be just that: passive. It should not require a huge time expenditure.

I bill my tenants through the mail using my software and then I watch the rents come in directly to my park account. I am able to balance the park books for my larger properties in about an hour per month. It takes me less than ten minutes to pay the park bills. This is all that is really required of a well-run park. And you will get here.

It has been years since I have even been to one of my more remote parks. Years. I have a wonderful team on site, the rents come in via direct deposit, we have a retired gentleman keep the park swept, and my jewel of an on-site manager takes care of the flower baskets. This park takes about thirty minutes per month of my time, to enter the rents and post the bills. I do my part by keeping the rents affordable for my retired tenants, who are on fixed income, and they have responded by maintaining a peaceful gorgeous setting. It is a beautiful, serene little park.

Unless you have significant repairs, which can be contracted out to subs, you are not going to spend a lot of time at your mobile home park. Most important is a reliable groundskeeper, so you are not needed for upkeep or picking up the odd piece of litter.

Your park rules require your tenants to maintain their own yards and landscaping, so all that is really left of you are park repairs, if even needed, and rent collection.

Mobile home parks are additionally easy to manage remotely because so much can be facilitated through mailing. U.S. Mail is still the most accepted and least challenged of all process-service in the courtroom. You are going to mail your invoices via first class mail. You are going to mail your notices via certificate of mailing.

When your rents start coming in, there are several techniques that work very well for tracking these online. First, choose your park located close to a bank that you use. Set up an individual park account specifically for the tenants. Next, charge the tenant their space rent, plus whatever cents their space is. For example, the tenant in space #1 pays $300.01, and the tenant in space #25 pays $300.25. You will also issue an accompanying deposit slip that these renters take to the bank to make their deposit.

Gone are the days of checks being "lost in the mail." You can log on instantly, and the tenant gets instant credit for his rent payment right on the day he paid, and the bank gives him a receipt! Additionally, write the tenant's space number on the deposit slip you send, so if you ever need to check who paid what rent, you will be able to log on and view that deposit slip with their space number.

On a property where you have passed through the water/sewer bill, print two copies of each tenant bill. Since each bill is a unique amount, keep a folder with all the bills near your computer. As rents appear in the bank account, locate the matching invoice. Since all are different, you know instantly who paid their bill. And again, if there is ever any question, you are able to crosscheck on the viewable deposit slip the bank also displays online.

The bank deposit idea is very convenient for tenants. They can go to any of the bank's locations surrounding the park. They can walk in or drive through and deposit cash, check or money order. The bank issues them their receipt for payment of rent, so the tenants leave the bank with proof they paid. Access to banks should be a consideration for you when you are looking at parks because it takes the work out of collecting your rents.

If you are purchasing a remote park, see if they have any type of office or outbuilding you can convert to an office. What you want to do then is set up a secured door with a mail slot. By allowing the tenants to deposit their rent payments through this door, you only have to come by once a month to collect your rents.

Make all rents due on the first. That way, you only have to come by on the eighth of the month. You can bring your notice pad with you as well, if you want to issue 72-hour notices for non-payment at that time. This is another example of a property that is only going to take about an hour of your time each month to run.

How many hours each month will you realistically spend running each park? My average per month is less than one hour per park on the nuts and bolts. I have one problem park in a really undesirable part of town, from which I deal with about one turnover per month, but I knew that going in. That is why I got such a good price on that property. Other than that, I invent beautification projects and schedule bids and repairs as needed.

There is one park in which I read my own water and sewer meters, and that adds another fifteen minutes per month but is worth the effort and time. I exchange fifteen minutes for $550 per month in recouped water expenses.

Your goal is to maintain a tidy, problem-free, well-run park so you have the freedom to come and go at your discretion, not the park's.

CHAPTER SIXTEEN
PAY YOUR OWN BILLS

It is very important that you pay your own bills. You need to have firsthand knowledge of where your park rents are being spent.

There are not going to be that many bills to keep track of. Your total bill-pay load will likely include city water/sewer, trash, electric, insurance, and your property taxes. There might be a few more depending on your particular park, but for the most part, you will have a small, manageable number of bills each month.

You do not get so far out of touch with your property that you are no longer knowledgeable about what is flowing in and out of your checkbook.

At a recent interview of another property I was researching, the sellers had assembled a team including their broker, family, my broker, and their on-site manager. The owners had not seen a bill from their park in years. As I worked through their manager's spreadsheets line by line, I could see the mounting horror on the owners' faces. There were whispers between the husband and wife, and soon they, too, were asking questions of the manager.

They had allowed the manager to run the park completely independently of their supervision, and she had done a splendid job in the eyes of the tenants. She bedecked the clubhouse with matching seasonal festive décor. She threw lavish parties every month and invited all the residents.

Meanwhile, the owners had not seen a profit in over five years. They were currently running at a significant loss.

My own experience with management paying my bills was equally upsetting. I had hired a manager for a small apartment complex I owned, and there were only several bills to be taken care of.

The bills came, and she never paid. Instead, she spent the money on herself, so when I became aware the bills still owed, there were no more rents available to cover them, and I had to pay them out of pocket. Worse, this had been going on for months. I was thousands in arrears on bills that bore my name. These were going straight for my perfect credit score.

I was able to keep all but one from reaching my credit. There was a $58 bill for the garbage that headed for collections. This $58 bill in collections ended up hurting my credit, something I have been fighting for years.

Sign your own checks, and pay your own bills. Always know what is going on financially inside your parks.

CHAPTER SEVENTEEN
UTILITIES

Park utilities are all the services coming into your park. Below-ground service providers include a combination of telephone, cable, and Internet providers, as well as gas, water, sewer, and electric companies. Above-ground services will include trash and debris removal, a dumpster if your site includes one, recycling and compost bins, possibly power if you have overhead lines, and a security provider if you utilize cameras.

Pay attention to what services you are paying for. This is critical to your bottom line. In an ideal situation, you will pay for *nothing*. You ideally do not want to be responsible for paying any utility bills. Here is why: You have a mortgage every month. You know what that number will cost you. You can control your rents, and your tenants must pay base rent. That is a given. That is all the control you have. You cannot go into their privately owned homes and make them fix that $2 flapper valve on their toilet that is skewing your water bill $1,000 per month.

There are some steps you can take to minimize your exposure to horrendous utility bills. This is so important, and it is the number one deal killer between parks that are successful and parks where the owners are losing money every single month. If you have not yet purchased the park, you need to list in your purchase agreement a contingency requiring a breakdown of all utilities paid by the owners. Additionally, require copies of all the bills, for at least the last two years. This will show you trends, leaks, and spikes if the bills are inconsistent.

Gather all the park's utility bills. Start your analysis. The first utilities you want to identify are all the *elective utilities*. Utilities that tenants *elect* to use are the easiest for you to eliminate from *your* bill. The tenant will then choose if they wish to continue that service on their own. You should not be paying a telephone or cable bill for anyone.

If you are considering a park with an on-site laundromat, you may see a small gas bill (around $18 per month for two washers and two dryers), but the laundry will pay for itself.

Next, analyze the park's electric bills. There may be a common areas light bill, but you should not be paying anyone's individual electricity bill. You do not have knowledge or control over what electrical appliances tenants are utilizing in their home, how many lights they leave on, or if they are growing medicinal marijuana plants that require bright lights. Always write it into your rental agreements that the tenant pays electric. When a tenant moves or gets evicted, it is that tenant's responsibility to contact the power company and shut off their bill. The new tenant moving in is responsible for switching the power into his own name.

The next utility you will come across is garbage. The park you are buying will already have garbage service. You need to find out who is paying this bill. If it is the park, you need to find out if it is can-service (every one rolls their own can to the curb for pick-up) or a common area dumpster. How much is the garbage bill costing each month? There is usually a significant cost increase if the garbage company has to empty individual garbage cans as opposed to emptying a dumpster.

The reason parks prefer individual cans is because you are able to "pass through" the utility expenses in a mobile home park after issuing 90-day's advance notice, and can-service is a very easy pass-through. After your 90-day notice, the garbage company discontinues sending you the bill and individually invoices your tenants.

The biggest deal breaker in buying any park is always the water/sewer bill. This is the number one reason parks are unprofitable. Tenants almost always own their own homes which means you have no idea to what extent that tenant is maintaining the interior of the residence. There may exist leaks and issues driving a water/sewer expense due to the tenant's negligence. If you are considering purchasing a park where the water and sewer are paid by the park, you need to take a critical look at that bill. This is an expense you can remedy, and turn your park very profitable.

Inquire with the city about installing sub-meters, which will allow you to monitor and charge each tenant for his individual usage, thus recouping your water/sewer bill. Often the city will quote you their price if you hired them to do the work, but will allow you to contract the work to a contractor other than the city. For example, on a recent sub-metering project my park's quote from the city was $5,100 per meter. I was able to work with a local contractor to meter the entire park for a total cost of $2,600 which was spread out over several months, since the contractor installed three meters per week. I paid him as he worked, giving him about $300 per week for just under nine weeks. This was easier on the park budget, and we were able to have the project completely debt free by the time he was finished.

After installing your sub-meters, issue a three-month notice (or whatever notice is required by your local statute) that you are executing a utility pass-through for the water and sewer bill. Each month, you or your staff will read the individual meters and pass through the actual usage to each home, so everyone pays their own actual usage. The bill for that park now averages $560, of which the tenants pay 100 percent. Cost savings to the park were between $3,000 to $4,000 per month, for a project that took us under three months to complete. This was a simple solution: the bank was delighted, and the tenants were thrilled to have control over their individual usage and bills instead of being hit with a rent raise to off-set their neighbor's water usage.

What utilities should you expect to encounter with a typical park of between 15 to 20 units?
- Common area lights: This number should range between $30-$65.
- Water bill: If you are on a well, monthly testing fees should be about $40
- If you are city water, ask how it is billed and what the city charges to sub-meter, or if they will allow you to sub-meter
- Sewer bill: If you are in the country, you will pay nothing because you are on septic. If you are hooked up to city sewer, find out if this bill is an integral part of your water bill; this takes care of itself when you sub-meter because the same number of units goes on the bill; you just charge the number of units times the city's two rates: one for water, one for sewer
- Trash: Call all the local service providers and compare rates. Ask what they would charge for can service and inquire about switching all your tenants over to their own garbage can bill; if individually-billed can service is not an option,

find out what they would charge you for monthly can service versus a weekly dumpster. Compare prices on all those and get the most affordable for you. My trash bills average $270 to $300 per month for each park I own.

CHAPTER EIGHTEEN
PARK RULES

Park rules are your tools when you go to court or get challenged to defend yourself in an eviction trial. When you sign a rental agreement with each tenant, present your renter with a copy of your park rules that he or she is required to live by. Your tenant does not have to sign these rules. Your tenant does not necessarily have to initial that he or she even received these rules for them to be binding. Visit your state's web site that has state required statutes on mobile home parks for your area. If possible, acquire a copy of the park rules if any have existed prior to your ownership.

You will want to structure your park rules in accordance with your state's statutes.

Address at least the following categories in your park rules:
- Definitions of terms used throughout your rules such as
- Homeowner, Space, and Landlord
- Mobile Home and Lot Maintenance
- Homeowners and Guests

- Subletting
- Utilities
- Pets
- Vehicles
- Firearms
- Partial Invalidity of Park Rules
- Termination of Lease / Rental Agreement

If there are no rules to be found and you are not comfortable writing new park rules from scratch, there are a working set of park rules that I use in my parks available for purchase and download to your computer, at www.MobileHomeParkInfo.com click on FORMS.

CHAPTER NINETEEN
BE STRICT

One of the biggest temptations when you own a mobile home park is to be everybody's best friend. Tenants are going to compare notes about different ways you have handled things, for example letting them skip a payment or not paying their park-billed utility bill. Tenants will get away with every single thing you let them get away with, and then you will be in a weak position because you already let someone else get away with the same thing. This is a terrible situation to find yourself in.

You must be strict and you must be consistent. Once you start to slide on your notices, it is almost impossible to catch a renter up. In fact, that renter can use your own kindness against you by showing the judge that they have a history of being late, and you have a history of allowing it. Once you have allowed deviation for one tenant, you must allow it for every tenant.

You will need to issue them a letter to correct your mistake, something formal to protect yourself legally, along the lines of, "We may have accepted late rents in the past. This is not our policy. Please pay this amount by this date to avoid late fees and 72-hour notice."

Being strict makes the good tenants happy because they feel they are residing in a park with order, where offenders are not tolerated. Take action and be consistent. Do not allow behaviors that could be construed as reverse discrimination.

Be compassionate, but keep in mind your inaction may be used against you in court. Be strict and consistent with issuing your notices.

CHAPTER TWENTY
COLLECTING RENT

This chapter is all about collecting the rents you are owed. Rent collection is nothing to be embarrassed about. You are running a business. Collecting rents is your job. Renters have entered a contractual agreement to pay you your monthly rents, and the bank has loaned you money with the understanding and expectation that you will be able to collect on those obligations to make your loan payments.

Renters that are not paying you are essentially stealing from you. They are breaking their contract, and they are forcing you to deal with them if you want your rent or your space back to rent to someone else. They are putting you in a compromising situation with your lender. There may be a legitimate reason why the renter is late, and you will have to weigh the excuses if you start accepting late rent and making exceptions. The positive side is that if someone really is between jobs or dealing with a catastrophic event in his or her life, then you have the flexibility and compassion to deal with those renters on a case-by-case basis.

Be careful with deviating from due dates and accepting late rents. Renters talk among themselves, and pretty soon half your park may have a tough-luck story for you. Maybe you have befriended a few renters and are dismayed that those are the ones who are chronically late. Honest tenants are not going to give you a bad time about paying you rent. They appreciate being there, and they are happy you are their landlord.

There are several ways to collect rents. Look at how your park is set up. Do you have an office location that can be secured, with an office door through which you can install a secure mail slot? This is one way for you to accept rent from your park. You simply show up on the eighth of the month and collect your rents from your secure mail drop; if you bring several 72-hour blank notices with you, these can be written at the same time you make sure everyone has paid.

Only use this system if you are in a safe area and can absolutely secure your office. Require renters to pay with check or money order only. Do not accept cash if you are having them drop rents through a mail slot. If word got out that there was $6,000 cash sitting on the other side of that door, it would not be long before someone found a way in.

The most fail-safe way I have found to collect rent is to mail individual invoices each month to each tenant and have them direct deposit their rent into a park account that I have established just for the tenants at that park at a bank nearby. Inside the tenant's bill, which you mail, enclose a deposit slip for that free account that only your tenants make deposits into, which you set up for that park in Chapter 6. By linking your main park account that you pay bills from, you can "sweep" your rent money safely into your own park account that tenants have no access to. Choose a bank that is within a half-mile of the park, so even the renters without cars have the ability to travel there by walking or bus.

The renters then drive-through or walk into whichever bank you have made this arrangement with, and deposit their rent using the deposit slip you have mailed them. The bank hands them a stamped and dated receipt. Their rent shows up in the park account instantly, and you can log on from wherever you are and see that they have paid. This system is fast and easy, and it works on many levels. No more lost rents, and no disputes if they say they paid but there is no record on your bank statement.

If you are concerned about having so many rents of the same amount that you do not know which spaced paid, or perhaps they lost their deposit slip and used a teller counter deposit slip, then just assign an odd number of cents after the space. For example, if every tenant pays $425 for rent, then assign space #1 a rent of $425.01, space #2 a rent of $425.02, and so on.

By mailing rent-due invoices you created through your rent tracking program, such as one of the Quickbook programs, you now have a way to charge and collect for your pass-through utility billing. For example, if you are reading water / sewer meters, you pre-load the city charges for that service so when you enter the tenant's usage, for example 2.6 units x the rates, then it extends and automatically calculates the tenant's usage. So, the fist line on your invoice is their space rent, so you enter for example: space #1 and your program will pull up whatever you are charging space #1, 400.01 and then next line, her utility usage 2.6 units of water / sewer x the rate and that total is what the tenant owes you for the month. You have just billed them for rent and a pass-through utility.

If you have other pass-through utility charges, put them all on one bill, and the total owed by each tenant will be unique amounts each month making it easy for you to log onto your bank account and check who has paid you yet. Print yourself a duplicate copy of all the renter bills you have just issued, so you can quickly reference through your invoices and match the bill with the amount that has just shown up in the park bank account.

If you are partnering with any local women's shelters or abuse-prevention programs placing protected renters, you may be receiving payments from third parties such as a county or city agency, or a church group or St. Vincent de Paul. The agency will work with you directly to arrange payment, and usually pay a bulk amount upfront to place the individual, and they will want an itemized bill upfront of all the fees they need to pay for this tenant to move in: space deposit, key deposit if you have locked fencing or security gates, screening and application fee, criminal background check fee, cleaning fee (stipulate if this is refundable or non-refundable), and whatever fees you are charging upfront for someone to move into your park. Likely the agency will want to pay several months ahead, and at some point stipulate after that the tenant should convert to a private pay who is then responsible for paying her own rent.

If you have decided to accept Section 8 tenants, this situation usually involves a unit that you own that you designate Section 8 housing and it will be inspected yearly. You will need to verify with your local HUD or find out who in your area is overseeing this federal funding program for lower-income renters. Section 8 direct-deposits the bulk of your rent payment directly into your bank account. This does not need to be the same account your tenants use, if you wish it to deposit directly into your park bill paying account. The program is very safe and it will be a government entity depositing into your account. Section 8 in your area will have a free website that you can list your vacancies on if you want units in your park to be part of this program.

Some of your disabled renters may have payees out of town that pay their bills for them, so you are still going to receive rents through the mail. You cannot mandate this direct-deposit system, and some renters are going to be very old-fashioned about how they have always paid and will insist on mailing you a check.

If you do not already have one, you will want to rent a P.O. Box. At NO time should your renters *ever* have your personal home address or know where you live. This is a safety issue. You will want to either conduct your business at your property, or meet tenants at a neutral public location.

If you know a tenant is going to be mailing you a rent check, enclose a self-addressed envelope. You do not need to put a stamp on it, but at least enclose a payment envelope for his or her convenience. It really increases your chances of getting that check in the mail, and your renter will really appreciate it.

If a tenant calls and says he or she wants to pay cash, you might consider meeting as soon as possible, with your receipt book.

CHAPTER TWENTY-ONE
NOTICES:
What Happens When Tenants Fail To Pay Rent

Issuing notices is an unpleasant task that accompanies mobile home park ownership. When a tenant does not pay rent, several questions to ask yourself are:

- Is it the first time they have been late?
- Is this tenant late every single month?
- Do you want to find out what the problem is?
- Do you have any interest in working with this tenant and retaining them in your park?

If you have determined that this tenant is simply not going to be paying you rent this month, it is time to issue a notice.

To simplify your bookkeeping, make your rents all due on the first of each month. Tenants have a grace period after which the rents are late. If your rents come due the first, the soonest, in most places, you can safely issue a valid notice for non-payment of rent is on the eighth of the month. Verify this by referencing your state's statute.

The notice you will use is called a **72-Hour Notice To Vacate For Non-Payment of Rent**. This means the tenant has 72 hours until the expiration date on your notice to pay the rent. On the notice, you will stipulate how and where you will accept that rent, so there is no confusion with the tenant saying rent was mailed when you told them to put it through the office door. If the rent does not show up where or when you stipulate payment, you file your notice. The tenant did not pay under the terms of the notice.

You can find sample notices on the Internet, but the safest idea is for you to join your local chapter of Manufactured Housing Communities. Once you become a member, you are able to purchase up-to-the-minute legal forms that have been drafted by lawyers and professionals that deal only with mobile home park law. This language that is already built into the form from the housing community will help your notice stand up in court.

It is extremely critical that you write a "good" notice. "Good" simply means your notice will stand up in court. If you are not sure what a notice that will hold up in court looks like, fax it to your lawyer and have him or her read it through. It is worth your time to do this if you have any questions.

Next comes the question of service. How are you going to serve your notice on your tenant? There are several ways that mobile home park landlords do this, and I have lost in court on every single one. I cannot stress to you enough how important "good" service is in order for you to win your eviction.

Here are your choices for "good" service:
- Mail via certificate of mailing
- Nail (means post it on the tenant's door)
- Nail and Mail
- Process serve via licensed process server
- Serve via your private investigator
- Serve via your local sheriff
- Serve it yourself by handing to tenant

There are several additional notices you have in your arsenal for eviction. You will want to either find examples on the Internet of these notices, or you can purchase a pad of each blank notice from your local manufactured housing community.

The first is a **24-Hour Notice To Vacate**. You can use a 24-hour notice under the following circumstances:

- <u>Imminent threat</u>:   the tenant, tenant's guest, someone in the tenant's control, tenant's pet, threatened   seriously   to   cause   substantial personal injury, or threatened to inflict any significant personal injury on another person on the premises other than on you
- <u>Reckless endangerment</u>:   the tenant recklessly endangered someone else on the premises, other than you, by causing a serious risk of injury
- <u>Inflicting substantial personal injury</u>: this could be caused by the tenant, someone in the tenant's control, or the tenant's pet
- <u>Intentional damage</u>:   caused   by   tenant,   or   a repeat substantial damage caused by tenant's pet
- <u>Committing an act outrageous in the extreme</u>: this could be caused by the tenant, someone in tenant's control, or tenant's pet. Outrageous acts could include a variety or activities, such as

making drugs, prostituting, bullying, breaking into a neighbor's home

- The tenant moving another party into his home after tenant has vacated: if you have not knowingly accepted rent from the new tenant, you can issue a 24-hour eviction to remove the new resident
- Tenant providing false information on his application for tenancy: you have one year to use this

In instances where you are issuing this notice for pet offenses, the tenant may have the right to dispose of the animal and cure your 24-hour notice, depending on the state where you live. In certain states, repeat offenses by the pet cannot be cured by removing the animal from your park.

The biggest misconception about 24-hour notices is that the tenant must be off your premises in 24 hours. What the 24-hour notice means for you is that you have terminated their tenancy, and now have to wait 24 hours to file it with the court if they remain.

The next notice you will use in your evictions is called a **30-Day Notice To Vacate For Cause**. This is a pretty big gun. You do not have to start with this notice. If a tenant is violating one of your park rules, start by talking with him or her. Your tenant might not have even realized he or she was doing anything wrong or offensive to others. They might even have a good reason. If talking to them does not solve the problem, you can send them a lesser notice. Examples of notices that are not quite as serious as a 30-day notice include: parking violations, pet violations, clean- up notices, maintenance on their home, and notices of disturbance.

If your written notice does not cure the problem, it is time to send a shot across the bow in the form of a 30-day for cause notice. Basically, this notice informs the tenant that you will terminate their tenancy if they do not correct the cause of the notice within 30 days. This gets most tenants attention. They will usually call you at this point and figure out how to correct their violation. If the tenant does not cure the cause of your notice, your next step is to file your 3-day notice in FED court.

If the tenant shapes up for thirty days but then starts violating again for the same offense any time in the next six months, then it is time to issue a 20-day notice. The 20-day is exactly like the 30-day, except this time they have to move. There is no curing a 20-day notice after you have served a valid 30-day notice to vacate for cause on the tenant.

Be careful to write a "good" notice that will hold up in court. Proper service is critical to your eviction process. Your types of notice will include 72-hour, 24-hour, 30-day for cause, and various lesser notices.

CHAPTER TWENTY-TWO
GOING TO COURT
FEDs And Trials

When you file an eviction, you start a centuries old process called Forcible Entry and Detainer, or FED for short. Basically, this is you terminating the lease with the tenant and getting your premises back so you can rent again.

FED promises one thing to the landlord: prompt relief. For this reason, the court process has been streamlined through the system. When you take your notice to court for the first time, you will fill out that court's eviction packet and pay filing fees. Before you leave, you will be assigned a court date for first appearance.

Since you are already in the courthouse, most courts assume you are going to have the sheriff serve your FED notice. You will either need to do this before you leave or make sure the court is getting this to the sheriff for you.

Because the entire eviction process is accelerated in court time, it is very important that you can show you have an indisputable, unequivocal right to possession of that space. This is where your "good" notice and proper proof of service are going to be key. You will need to be able to prove both.

The date of first appearance arrives. You are either representing yourself, or you have hired council. At this point you do not really need to hire an attorney if you are keeping your costs down.

Courts reward those who try to work it out. Some courts will even have a free mediator available if you choose to go that route. Your choices at this point of first appearance are simple:

- Speak with the tenant and negotiate a move-out date and terms under which you wish the move to happen. You and the tenant will then present this agreement to the judge. He will ask both parties if that is their signature, and he will sign it into order.
- If negotiations are not going smoothly, request the mediator to help you write a mutually acceptable agreement. This mediator's agreement will be what you present to the judge, or else the mediator will go back with you

before the judge and explain why the parties are not coming together.

- If talks are hostile and proceeding poorly, then your tenant may demand a trial. If he or she does so, your tenant must pay trial fees the same day or get a note from the court that fees are waived until the date of the trial. At this point, you also need to go pay trial fees.

- If your dispute with the tenant is over something other that non-payment of rent, you may have already signed a mandatory arbitration agreement in your lease if you used the manufactured housing community lease form. At this point, your disagreement would reroute to an arbitrator.

Some FED proceedings leave little room for argument on the part of the tenant because the notice is not able to be cured. Such notices include:

- 30-Day No Cause Notice: this notice may be issued to travel trailers, fifth-wheel trailers, RV's, or apartment dwellers only. The only defense for a 30-Day No Cause is retaliation on the part of the landlord. Otherwise, this is an incurable eviction notice.

- 30-Day Notice For Cause Under the Three Strikes Law: in some states, if you issue three 72-hour notices for non-payment of rent within a 12-month period, you are allowed, after the third notice (but since this could be argued because it is still a new law with gray areas, safely after the fourth notice), to invoke the three-strikes law. Once you issue this, there is *no cure* and your tenant must vacate. If you have any questions at all about the legitimacy of your notices, it is prudent to have all of them reviewed by your counsel.

Being proactive about issuing notices will result in fewer trials. This will save you time, money, and grief over the long run. Make yourself as defendable as possible, by using 30-day no cause and the three-strikes' notice-system whenever possible.

Filing FED's and going to trial is costly. Serve the most defensible notices you can; more notices will lead to fewer trials.

CHAPTER TWENTY-THREE
PROBLEMS IN YOUR PARK

One of the unexpected side effects of park ownership is that you are not only going to meet persons from all walks of life, but you are also walking part of the journey with them, as they go through some of the most difficult transitions in their lives.

You are not necessarily going to be seeing these individuals at their best. You might be meeting them at one of the most challenging times in their life. They could be getting evicted, going through divorce (and they obviously did not get the house), undergoing the stress of moving, losing a spouse, loved one, or pet, or even themselves dying.

Be understanding and be sympathetic. Just be supportive of your tenants' needs because the tenant is your customer.

The challenge comes when your customers do not get along with each other.

Park communities are a grand-scale family dynamic, and your role is to effectively, with as little bias and drama as possible, get all the members to cohabit peacefully. In fact, it is not only your job, but in my state it happens to also be the law. You are ultimately liable if they are not peaceful. The right to peaceable enjoyment is the given right of tenants.

You will very quickly want to sort out the nonsense. You do not want to waste time with the gossip or neighbor-to-neighbor disputes. Be careful of one neighbor trying to take out or eliminate another neighbor just because they do not like them. You will be manipulated if this ends up being the case, and the disgruntled party that you did not side with may try to sue you for anything they can think of – maybe alleging a fair housing violation, or retaliation – even though you have done nothing wrong except you tried to wade into a situation between neighbors. Civil disputes must be resolved between the parties without you; you do not even want to get dragged into who said what. It will have blown over in a few days any way, or they need to call the police and get themselves into neighborhood mediation which is free to them and impartial.

If it is a real estate issue about the size of someone's yard, you can divide the yards according to your state fire code. This may not necessarily mean splitting the yards down the middle between the homes. In some situations, fair yards grandfathered into fire code do not mean the parties split the yard 50-50. Rather, the person who has been there the longest gets to measure from whatever point hangs out the closest to the new neighbor, and they split *that* distance 50-50.

If you encounter an offender who is outside your park who is bothering your tenants and just plain does not like being neighbors with a park, you can start by encouraging dialogue and good will. If this is simply not an option, your tenants may involve law enforcement for more serious transgressions, such as vandalism or peaceful disturbance. If no police reports are generated, you can keep track of the incident numbers on the neighborhood offender. Judges understand jail overcrowding, and if you have enough incident numbers, it carries enough weight after awhile with some judges as an actual citation.

Overall, your park will be a very enjoyable community that turns itself into a family. Even though the dynamics between tenants are going to be as different as their personalities, you will see many tenants looking out for one another and building a real community with block parties and neighborhood barbeques and taking meals to those who might be home bound. You can also encourage comradery by hosting a monthly lunch or potluck get-together.

You can designate a communication board maybe located by the park mailboxes, where tenants can post fliers and community service announcements or invitations to get-togethers.

At one park where I kept a central office, we had a trip planned every month of the year to a different destination such as a local casino, or on a wine tasting tour. We would figure out the cost per person, maybe $20 to $50 dollars for the day, depending on how many signed up, and this would cover the cost of a limousine, lunch, and admission for whoever had signed up for the trip.

Because we had so many tenants volunteering around the property, planting flowers and sorting mail, and helping around the office, I would also hold a monthly volunteer luncheon honoring our helpers.

You may have several tenants that will want to complain to you, but overall you will discover and cultivate a positive park environment where you steer clear of rumblings or discord between individual tenants, and intead focus on the positive activities that tenants can enjoy together.

CHAPTER TWENTY-FOUR
KEEPING YOUR PARK FULL AND PROFITABLE

Empty spaces and vacancies in your park are a huge source of lost revenue. After safety in your park, keeping your park full should be your top priority. You need to keep your park full or you are leaving money on the table. You will never see that revenue again. Vacant spaces are such an easy issue to fix.

Start by researching your market, which you probably already did when you purchased your park.

- Who are your tenants?
- Where do they work?
- What do they do for income?
- What is their average household take home pay?
- Even if you are surrounded by gas stations, convenience stores, and fast food, these are ideal future tenants for your park. At any given moment, how many young adults are trying to move out of their parents' home and get established on their own?

- Are there elderly persons in your area, trying to maintain their independence but with less maintenance than in a home-ownership situation?
- Are there disabled persons wishing to exit a group home or disadvantaged living situation, yet are capable of independent living in your park?

If you are considering renting to persons in transition, you may wish to contact your local women's or men's homeless shelters.

Sadly in this economy, a very real contingent in our communities now are homeless, unaccompanied youth; teens and young adults who are transient and finding themselves without either of their parents, living in someone else's home. I rent to everyone in transition. For me, it is all about providing safe, affordable housing, and getting homeless people off the streets into a stable place they can call home; that opportunity might change their lives for the better forever.

What you have to offer is safe, affordable living, and there is always a demand in every community.

The fastest and easiest way to keep your park full is to advertise:

- Start by putting up a For Rent notice on or near your mobile home park signage. This will cost you next to nothing. Your sign can simply say: FOR RENT and list your phone number. If you have purchased your park in an area where squatters are a concern, do not list the space number and arrange to meet potential renters in person with an application before disclosing the space.

- You can also run an ad on

  http://www.craigslist.com

  at no cost to you. If these options do not net you applicants, some other affordable options are to contact your local housing authority and see if they have a web site where landlords advertise vacancies. This is also free advertising for you.

- Word of mouth is another option for you to advertise at no cost to you: do any of your tenants have relatives or friends they are willing to refer who want to apply for the vacancy in your park. You can encourage referrals by offering to waive the application fee for applying, if you are willing to waive this, since you know you will recoup that $40 screening charge via recaptured rent versus the vacancy, if you rent to this individual.

- Next, if you still have a vacancy after exhausting the no cost means, you might consider listing your vacancy in a local community circular such as the Nickel Ads or a local community guide. The cost of a small ad averages about $5 and comes out every other week. Some of these publications enjoy a large, free distribution base and will reach many of your out-lying areas.

- Your local paper will have a place for you to also advertise your vacancy. Ask about rates and specials. Even in the more expensive papers, you will be able to find ads for reduced rates by inquiring about specials and ways to shave costs off the ad. Ask the classifieds department what day of the week all the rentals come out. Do not assume that this comprehensive rental listing day comes out on the weekend, or even in the big Sunday paper. In some small towns, the rental ads present on Fridays. You will just want to ask and at least put your ad in for that one day to get the most impact for your advertising dollar.

Now I am going to share my best technique with you that has proven to be the secret to keeping all my parks full with waiting lists: selling park-owned trailers on contracts. If you have a vacancy and have not received any applicants that have their own unit, you might consider that potential renters who want to live in your park may not be able to afford to purchase their own home. For whatever reason – divorce, lost employment, spotty credit history—they are unable to even qualify for a trailer purchase through a conventional dealer. Dealer costs and interest rates are exorbitant, and added fees include transport and set up of the unit.

Here is where you have a huge advantage. You own the home court. Look at the space you are trying to rent, and determine what size trailer will fit in that space. Is your vacant space sized for a single-wide or double-wide manufactured home? If so, you want to research putting a home in this space and becoming the bank yourself – I am talking about selling the manufactured home on contract to a new tenant. This is known as park-owned financing.

At this point, you are probably thinking to yourself, how am I going to afford to pay out of pocket for a single- or double-wide home, when mobiles cost anywhere from $3,000 all the way up to $170,000 per mobile home? Surprisingly, I have often located FREE single- and double-wide homes on craigslist.

Especially in areas where new home construction is higher, often home builders or their contractors will set up a temporary situation in a mobile home, that has to be physically removed from the property as soon as the new home construction is complete.

By visiting

http://www.craigslist.com

again and researching manufactured homes in various areas, I believe you will be surprised at the number of units available for reduced or no cost except the expense of moving the home.

Depending on where you are looking, the last several times I have looked on craigslist for a manufactured home, I have found anywhere from one to six FREE homes that have to be moved.

The person listing the home will give you the home for free or for next to nothing if you will come haul it away. In a lot of these situations, the mobiles are nicer and include a number of appliances. Again, it was likely a situation where the home owner was building their dream home in the country, and their local county allows them to set up a manufactured home to reside in temporarily until the new construction has been finalized and passed its finish inspection. At this point, the homeowner has to disable, and in some cases completely remove, the temporary home, or they will be fined.

Other situations where I have encountered nearly new mobile homes that were free to whomever would move them were scenarios in the county where a neighbor had turned in another neighbor for renting or housing a tenant or family member in a home that had been placed without permits. The property owner was going to be fined $1,000 per day until the mobile home structure was removed.

In another free mobile home situation, the owner had placed the structure, again without permits, and a neighbor driving by had reported the new wedding planning business being operated from the structure. This owner then placed the home on craigslist free to anyone that would come remove it before the county fines started. The home included a pellet burning stove, new washer and drier, and a brand new oven. Additionally they had remodeled inside and it also had three bedrooms and came with a bar.

There is also the potential of getting the new manufactured home moved for absolutely free. In your area, there are likely organizations set up, non-profits and 501C charity organizations that are interested in helping homeless people find permanent housing. Researching such programs may benefit you and provide you cost savings to partner with a local organization to place this free trailer in your park, especially if you are intending to work with persons coming from distressed or homeless situations, or are an emergency agency placement, for example if someone is being hidden or placed by a case worker, away from an abusive partner.

The next step, once you have the dwelling placed in your park, is to work with the buyer on a payment plan. Even though you found the home for free, it has value and you need to recapture the time and expense you have in that home. Be fair with your market value and share that good deal with your tenant. There are several ways to determine market value on the home. You can research your local real estate listing service and local listings of similar homes to see what the local market price is. Next, you can contact the county where you set the home up in and find out what the county believes the tax-assessed value is on that home.

Once you have established a sales price, you will want to use a professional form such as the Retail Installment Contract (Form No. 1204 for Motor Vehicles, Trailers, and Mobile Homes, available from Steven's Ness) for your installment sale. In addition to executing this agreement with your new tenant, you also need to visit an amortization web site and print out the payment schedule which will show the sales price, the interest rate you are charging, and the number of months the contract will extend. A good Web site for this is

http://www.bankrate.com

Print a copy of this chart for your buyer and keep a copy for yourself in a file with your buyer's contract for the home they are purchasing from you.

Another very cost-effective alternative for keeping your spaces full if you do not have the money or availability of a single- or double-wide manufactured home is to research the possibility of moving in a travel trailer.

Travel trailers, or coaches, or recreational vehicles are a very attractive idea to a lot of renters in transition. If the renter is only looking for something temporarily, the idea of buying a travel trailer on contract has merit because it affords them housing for the moment, and after they pay off the unit, they own it outright and can always take it on a road trip, or travel, or park it in the driveway of their future permanent home should they buy a stick built in their future.

Your tenants like the idea of building equity in the place they live in: a travel trailer will always belong to them, long after they pay it off. They do not always have to live in it, but they will always have the option to keep it or sell it.

If you are worried about a tenant driving off with your trailer in the middle of the night before it is paid for, you can lock a padlock onto the trailer hitch where the post or stand comes down from the hitch. There is a place for a padlock that only you will have the key to, and you or your manager can lock that leg straight down so the trailer cannot be towed until they have paid you off for the unit.

When a prospective tenant purchases a travel trailer from you, you have the added benefit that you are not responsible for their wear and tear or any maintenance on the home. They buy as-is.

The best places for you to buy a travel trailer, coach, or recreational vehicle to resell in your park, are at local repossess auctions or through an auction dealer. Check your local resources or start asking around at RV dealerships if they have a buyer who goes to auction.

Depending on your state, you may not be allowed to preview the auction trailer. Stricter laws have prevented unlicensed non-dealers from perusing the lot. But you can be on the phone with your dealer during the auction. He will have a chance to be your eyes before the auction, and you can be present via phone as he bids on the units you have designated. After auction, you have about 36 hours to approve or disapprove of the trailer. Check with the dealer and the auction house, know your rights, and adhere to all deadlines. Trailers purchased through the auction yard can be financed through your lending source, in the same manner as buying any car through a car dealer. It is best to have your financing lined up before auction, and be prepared to pay after the auction. Again, you can likely finance this purchase through your own lender.

Travel trailers are very easy to transport. You can often do this with your own SUV or truck. Depending on your local ordinances, you can likely transport a trailer or 5th wheel up to 40 feet in length. If the plates or stickers are not current, you will want to stop by your local Department of Motor Vehicles for a trip permit before moving the unit, or the trip permit may be included as part of your purchase package if you were working through an auction dealer.

Another great source for travel trailers, if you do not want to hassle with the auction, is again visiting

http://www.craigslist.com

by doing a search for recreational vehicles. You will find hundreds of listings in a variety of price ranges.

Another great source is your local newspaper, or the newspaper local to your mobile home park if you have purchased a park that is not near your home.

If you have a prospective tenant, you can ask the tenant to shop as well. Especially if the tenant is anxious to move into your park and putting pressure on you to hurry up and find them a unit, you may wish to suggest they actively search as well on finding a unit that might work for their budget and monthly payment scenario.

Financing a travel trailer can be achieved through a local bank or likely through whatever banks you have maintained a banking relationship with. By shopping a variety of banks for this transaction, you will succeed in securing yourself the lowest, longest-term interest rate possible. You will want to charge at least a couple interest points over this when you resell the home.

If the tenant was arranging their own financing, local lenders, if the tenant could even find financing, might charge the tenant anywhere from 29.99 to 35.99 percent interest on the loan for the unit.

You are more likely to find 6.9 to 8.5% financing for yourself if you finance the unit purchase through your bank.

By turning around and selling that unit at an interest rate that is agreeable to you and beneficial to your tenant, you might offer the tenant park financing in the range of 16 percent interest, or whatever you work out.

This arrangement is a profit to you, and a benefit to your tenant who can now pay you a monthly payment along with their space rent.

For example, if you purchase a unit for $5,000 at 7.9% interest, your monthly payment amortized over 5 years will be $101. It the tenant were to find their own financing, they would likely be paying more for the same unit, for example $8,500, and their financing with the 29 to 35 percent interest charge would be $307 monthly payment.

However, if your park sells the tenant the same unit, now for $8,500 because you are going to sell the units for more than you acquire them for, at a 16% interest rate financed by your park, then the tenant's monthly payment to you is $208.

This monthly payment over the next 5 years will capture you over $4000 in interest income to you, plus the $3,500 profit that you netted from the sale of the $5,000 unit for $8,500. Your interest on the underlying loan of 7.9% on a $5,000 unit is a little over $1,000 over the same time frame. So if this scenario is something you are considering, you would have acquired a long term – at least 5 year – tenant, and netted $6,500 additional dollars in addition to the monthly rent you are receiving from this tenant.

In one situation, I purchased a mobile home park with a tenant living in a burned out trailer, unknown to me or anyone. He kept it a secret. Although trailer looked cosmetically fine on the outside, the inside stunk and was black char and burn. But the tenant did not have insurance, resources or credit to make costly repairs or replace his unit; unknown to even the sellers, this tenant had been living in this burned out shell before I bought the park.

One day I happened to walk by as he was opening his door, and the inside of the home was horrifying and the smell was terrible.

I was able to find him a unit that had originally cost $90,000 but was being sold at the foreclosure auction for $15,900. In this case, I sold him the home for what I paid at auction for it to help him out since I did not feel his burned home was even habitable or safe. He had already resided in the park for 9 years, so I knew he would be a good long-term tenant. This tenant was employed by a road contractor so he had the income to cover a $263.00 monthly payment and he never paid late.

A scrap metal hauler paid him $500 for his old trailer, so he was able to get a fresh start.

Several months after moving into this new home, sadly this tenant passed away from cancer. But his final months were happy as he was ecstatic with the new home.

After his passing, the family decided to not want to move or keep the home, so they turned it back over to the park where the unit was resold on a new park contract.

Once you move a new park-owned trailer into your park, you are going to become the bank. Even though you may have gotten a good price on the new unit, you will want to establish a sales price that is closer to market price for your new trailer. You can go online and research the unit and what it would normally sell for by visiting:

http://www.nada.com

Once you have established the price for which you are selling the trailer, you may want to visit a stationary store for a contract sales form, such as the Steven's Ness Retail Installment Contract, consumer paper Form No. 1204, for the installment sale of Motor Vehicles, Trailers, and Mobile Homes. Next, you will need to run an amortization schedule on the new sales agreement at any mortgage web site. For this I use the calculators for either mortgage payment calculator or Loan and amortization calculator at:

http://www.bankrate.com

You will want to print out the interest and principal payment schedule. This will include the sales price, interest rate you are charging, and the number of months the contract will run. Keep a copy in your file and provide a copy of this payment schedule for your buyer. You will want to research which laws apply in your state with regards to this sale. Additionally, you may wish to see if any new federal legislation such as the Dodd-Frank financial reform bill applies to your sales depending on how many and what type of transactions you are doing or if you are titling permanent structures, manufactured homes, through a third party.

You might find that travel trailers, or coaches, or recreational vehicles will be the exception for you since those transactions involve vehicles that are not permanent because they have wheels under them and are not permanently set or skirted into your park.

Once you have established the sale, you will initiate your new tenant protocol. This will likely happen as follows:

-your new tenant fills out an application to rent in your park
-you charge them a screening fee
-you screen them through your tenant network screening service, private investigator, or local law enforcement
-once you have approved your tenant, you give your tenant your welcome letter with your park policy, dimensions of his or her new space, copy of your park rules
-your new tenant signs a rental agreement with your park for month to month tenancy for manufactured dwelling space or RV space

Tenants are often very grateful for the opportunity to purchase and take ownership of their own home. Affordable housing in your mobile home park builds tenants' self esteem, sets them on an affordable monthly budget, grants them home ownership, and builds their equity in their own home.

The pleasant and unexpected upside to this system is that you will develop waiting lists for your park. Banks are delighted when they discover you have not experienced a vacancy factor for years, using this system to keep your park full, with a waiting list of potential renters.

CHAPTER TWENTY-FIVE

STEP-BY-STEP INSTRUCTIONS:
Checklist For Buying Your Mobile Home Park

These final pages are your quick-reference checklist condensed for your convenience now that you are ready to buy your mobile home park.

☐ **Interview at least ten banks and find one that offers a free small business checking account.**

> ☐ Open a new account, into which you and your tenants are going to deposit all rents.
>
> ☐ Connect some overdraft protection to this account, in case a tenant ever bounces a rent check.
>
> ☐ Purchase deposit slips and print checks for this account.
>
> ☐ If you feel it is necessary, open one more account to sweep your rent money into if you are worried about fraud protection.

☐ **Set up your LLC.**

> ☐ Register your new business name.
> ☐ Mail in your payment to the state.

☐ Set up your business.

☐ Install or create on your office computer your rent management plan where you will track all your rents; you can use Quicken Rental Property Manager combined with QuickBooks Pro for invoicing, or you can make your own spreadsheets.

☐ Invest in a P.O. Box if you do not already have one; you do not want any disgruntled tenants knowing where you and your family reside.

☐ Line up your professional team of lawyers, bankers, realtors, screening company, process server, and private investigators if needed

☐ Contact your local Mobile Housing Community Chapter and interview them about joining; purchase rental agreement packets from your local chapter.

☐ Start shopping for mobile home parks at
http://www.mobilehomeparkinfo.com
http://www.loopnet.com
http://www.rmls.com

your local real estate listing service, and your local business classified listings section under Manufactured Parks For Sale.

☐ Compare as many parks as you can examine.

☐ Create files for each park examined.

☐ Analyze your choices based on the area in which you want to purchase and which parks are the lowest price for the highest number of spaces.

☐ **Narrow down your park selections.**

☐ Start crunching the numbers of each park based on cap rate (multiply the monthly rent times 12 months, minus taxes, divided by your purchase price: this number should be well above 12 percent which represents the percentage of return interest on your investment).

☐ Call your realtor to contact the seller or contact the selling agent yourself, and gather information about the rents and expenses to where you can analyze the cash flow of each park you have selected.

☐ **Get all your questions answered**; carefully reference the supplemental due diligence questions presented in Chapters 10 and 11, in addition to the many questions you can think of as well.

☐ **Talk to your realtor about writing an offer.**

☐ **Present your offer** and wait for acceptance, or counter the sellers offer accordingly.

☐ **Mark all your dates** for due diligence and performance on your calendar and complete each requirement timely.

☐ **Complete all your inspections** and release your contingencies, which are your list of criterion that must be satisfied by the sellers and property to your and your lender's sole satisfaction before funding the purchase of the park. Work closely with your buyers broker to see if there any additional matters that concern you during your due diligence period prior to removing your contingencies. If you are not completely satisfied, or if new questions have been raised that concern you, ask your broker to issue an addendum extending the time allotted you for inspection to your sole satisfaction.

☐ **Consult with your lender** regarding the time-line and when you are scheduled to close. Keep in good communication with your lender.

☐ **Sign and take possession.** For this step, your broker will have opened escrow and enlisted a title company where you will go to sign the papers for the transaction. If you are using a business lawyer to prepare the offer and sale, your legal council will be in communication with the title company to make sure your documents are in order. Negotiate how you wish the prorated rents and the prorated bills to occur. Some parties handle these matters outside of the oversight of the title company. This will be between you and your sellers if you wish the prorated rents to be paid into your column at close. If you are taking over a park at the beginning of the month, rents will likely come due on the 1st of the month so there will not be any prorated rents unless a tenant has paid ahead, at which point, you are owed that rent.

☐ **Issue introductory letter:** immediately after close, you will want to introduce yourself with your phone numbers and contact information so the tenants know how to pay their rent to you; it is also appropriate if you want the sellers to be the one to introduce you to the tenants, for the sellers to issue a letter of introduction on your behalf. You will want to include a letter of your park policies – with language such as "we are a family park that appreciates a drug free and safe environment for all tenants"; you may wish to execute new leases if there are any missing leases when you take over; and you will want to distribute your park rules (these do not have to be signed by the tenants to be binding; include the language that your park rules are an integral part of your rental agreement).

☐ **Keep yourself open to communication** from your tenants, especially if you are an off-site manager and do not plan on residing in your park.

In conclusion, there has never been a better time to take the steering wheel back and demand control of your own financial destiny.

Just to summarize, I believe that purchasing a mobile home park is the best investment in this and every economy, for the serious investor. I think every investor should consider owning at least one mobile home park, for the following reasons recapped:

- because parks enjoy a low to zero vacancy rate
- parks produce a steady stream of monthly income
- mobile home communities produce predictable monthly cash flow
- parks provide good return on investment
- you as the investor has control over cash flow and vacancy rate
- you as the park owner have additional opportunities to increase your monthly income and cash flow through rent raises, control of and reduction in your operating expenses, and by eliminating utility bills via pass-through billing
- Mobile home parks hold their market value and will typically appreciate in value

- There is always a demand for affordable housing found in parks
- You retain your initial nest egg that you purchased the park with – your investment dollars are in tact and available to you either by refinancing or selling your property to recapture 100% of your initial investment

My hope is that my twenty years of hands-on experience in the rental and mobile home park industry synopsized in this how-to manual has and will help guide your mobile home park investment experience.

I wrote my very first book about how to own a mobile home park for my friends who were all wanting to buy a park investment, and would ask me, how do you buy a park? I said, it might take me more than ten minutes to answer your question – let me write you a step-by-step guide.

I also lived in a mobile home park for 3-1/2 years until my early 20's before I started investing. My single-wide mobile was beautiful with vaulted ceilings, a real stone entry way, hardwood floors, and a grand piano.

Mobile home living can truly be an enjoyable experience, for you and for your tenants who are the lifeline of your new investment. I have one tenant who pays his rent by modeling his trailer and letting trade publications photograph how he has designed and decorated his space in all black and white checkerboards on the inside. His tattoos match and he blends in perfectly when they are photographed together.

I hope this guide, The New Investor's Guide To Owning A Mobile Home Park, has been helpful for your process. I do believe mobile home park ownership is the best investment in this economy. It just makes sense. And it just makes you money.

I now consider you one of my friends who wanted to know more about how to buy a park, and a fellow investor in mobile home parks. I believe you now have answers, solutions, ways to treat situations you might encounter, and that you hold the secrets to successful and profitable mobile home park ownership.

My hope is that your mobile housing community will prove to be your best investment alternative in this economic climate, and will be your most stable alternative investment for your future generations.

Mobile home parks have been the key to successful investing for many park owners and investors. Although it has been their well-kept secret, this investment reality is attainable by you.

You have an alternative that has worked for many who chose to exit the broken vehicle of the stocks and bonds market.

How many parks do you need to purchase? Since park investing involves economy of scale, you will likely want to purchase the park with as many spaces as you possible can, if those are in a strong rent producing area.

For some investors and sellers that I know, one park has filled the bill and was the only investment they ever needed. One park was all they have ever wanted to fulfill all their goals and dreams. In those cases, one investor owned a 44 space park where the rents averaged $350 per month so he was bringing in over $15,000 per month. Another seller owned a 78 space park that averaged space rents of about $235 so he was bringing in over $18,000 per month. And in another scenario, the park owner had a 55 space park that charged just under $600 per space, and she was bringing in about $32,000 per month. Rumor around her park was that one of Michael Jackson's giraffes found a good home on her estate. So one park might be all you ever buy, and that is just fine.

For other investors, buying multiple parks is a hobby and they get a well-oiled machine in place, using one park manager and a maintenance team to oversee a number of large parks in the same area.

Whether your choice is to move all your investment dollars into parks that you will buy and manage, or if you decide to simply add a single park on the side, in addition to your existing portfolio, and leave all your other investments in place, the choice of financial stability is up to you.

Fickle markets or the shifting tides of the local or global economies should no longer make you seasick, or dictate how much you risk, earn, or lose in your investment portfolio.

Mobile home park communities are a stable return on your investment, and they retain the value of your investment nest egg.

Mobile home park investing is your answer to transforming conventional fear-based investing into the long-term, stable, predictable investment you deserve which will in turn fund your own retirement.

Your financial future is up to you, and it looks great. You have the tools to achieving immediate returns on your investments, which are yours every single month for the rest of the time you own and profitably manage your own mobile home park investment.

Wishing you every success and all the best in your continued investment endeavors, as you now venture into the rewarding future of mobile home park investing!

Yours Sincerely,

Laura Cochran

CPSIA information can be obtained
at www.ICGtesting.com
Printed in the USA
LVOW04s2311010216

473249LV00016B/760/P